HIGH PERFORMANCE PRIVACY PRESERVING AI

JAYAVANTH SHENOY, PATRICK GRINAWAY
AND SHRIPHANI PALAKODETY

the essence of knowledge

Published, sold and distributed by:
now Publishers Inc.
PO Box 1024
Hanover, MA 02339
United States
Tel. +1-781-985-4510
www.nowpublishers.com
sales@nowpublishers.com

Outside North America:
now Publishers Inc.
PO Box 179
2600 AD Delft
The Netherlands
Tel. +31-6-51115274

ISBN: 978-1-63828-344-7
E-ISBN: 978-1-63828-345-4
DOI: 10.1561/9781638283454

Table of Contents

Acknowledgments

In addition to my coauthors listed, I also thank the rest of the team at Onai, particularly Guha Jayachandran and Galana Gebisa, for their assistance and support. The artwork was created by Jin-Ching Lim.

— Jayavanth Shenoy

DOI: 10.1561/9781638283454.ch1

Chapter 1

Introduction

Artificial intelligence (AI) depends on data. In sensitive domains – such as health-care, security, finance, and many more – there is therefore a tension between unleashing the power of AI and maintaining the confidentiality and security of the relevant data. This tension must be resolved for AI to reach its full potential in service of humanity.

Privacy-preserving techniques can enable AI while guaranteeing privacy. In this book we cover techniques, specifically secure multi-party computation (MPC) and homomorphic encryption (HE), that provide complexity theoretic security guarantees even with a single data point. These techniques have traditionally been too slow for real-world usage, and the challenge is heightened with the large sizes of today's state-of-the-art neural networks, including large language models (LLMs). We note that we do not in this book cover techniques like differential privacy that only concern statistical anonymization of data points.

The recent advances in AI were largely spurred by general purpose GPU (GPGPU) computing and innovation in distributed computing technologies. Fortunately, these same acceleration technologies can be brought to bear to accelerate secure MPC and HE too.

This book explains how advances in these three areas—AI, privacy-preserving techniques, and acceleration—allow us to achieve the dream of high performance privacy-preserving AI. It also discusses applications enabled by this emerging interplay.

The book begins with an overview of homomorphic encryption and secure MPC, explaining details of both at the level needed to understand the later discussion of acceleration, the challenges, and where the techniques should be utilized. The next part presents methods for acceleration, starting with hardware and proceeding to algorithmic specifics. We then proceed to a discussion of particular healthcare, drug discovery, and consumer applications enabled by the accelerated privacy preserving AI techniques presented. Lastly, we present methods for scaling to large numbers of untrusted participants with the use of additional cryptographic tools, notably blockchains and zero knowledge proofs.

Part I

Privacy Preserving Techniques

DOI: 10.1561/9781638283454.ch2

Chapter 2

Homomorphic Encryption

Homomorphic encryption (HE) is one technique that enables privacy-preserving computation. Operations (or circuit evaluations) are performed directly on homomorphically encrypted data. The result can then be decrypted. Since its introduction 46 years ago, homomorphic encryption has evolved significantly with a plethora of schemes to choose from, each with their own advantages and disadvantages. Following the invention of fully homomorphic encryption (FHE) in 2009, there has been a revolution in the field. FHE theoretically allows for evaluation of arbitrary circuits of unbounded depth. HE can be used with a variety of models, ranging from simple support vector machines (SVMs) and random forests to computationally expensive deep neural networks.

2.1 Introduction

This chapter introduces HE techniques and how they are used in privacy-preserving applications and especially in AI.

HE was first described by Rivest et al. [1] with four schemes: one for addition and subtraction; one for multiplication and test for equality (RSA [2]); and two for sum, difference, and products. Since then, there has been much work on developing systems that are feasible for real-world applications, including AI.

FHE allows evaluation of arbitrary circuits consisting of multiple types of gates (addition, subtraction, multiplication etc.) without needing decryption. The seminal paper by Gentry [3] introduced the first viable construction of FHE. Prior to that, there were other schemes that were close to achieving FHE, but they had key limitations. *Partially Homomorphic Encryption* schemes support evaluation of circuits of only one type of gate. *Somewhat Homomorphic Encryption* schemes can evaluate certain circuits with some types of gates (generally addition and multiplication). *Leveled Fully Homomorphic Encryption* schemes can evaluate arbitrary circuits of predetermined depth L, and support multiple gates types. Finally, *Fully Homomorphic Encryption* schemes support evaluation of circuits of unbounded depth, and also support multiple gate types. All of these schemes are discussed in more detail in Section 2.5. Since the Gentry's pioneering FHE work, several other FHE schemes have been introduced 2.6.

Currently, there are HE libraries written in several languages, including Rust, C, and C++, and there are bindings for many more. Most of the schemes described in these libraries are too slow for practical use in AI. The schemes that leverage accelerators to achieve speedup are described in Chapter 4. Applications of accelerated HE in AI are discussed in Chapter 5.

HE can be used either standalone or with other techniques like multi-party computation (MPC). Chapter 3 discusses some MPC schemes that use HE for circuit evaluation on encrypted data. Finally, Section 2.7 describes work on standardization of HE. As HE becomes mainstream, standardization is necessary to ensure that the schemes are secure and that the users adopting the schemes do so without introducing vulnerabilities.

2.2 Motivation

Homomorphic encryption is a cryptographic technique where computation can be performed on encrypted data. This is useful when computations have to be performed on secret data which cannot be revealed to anyone except the owner of the data. Hospitals, research laboratories, defense organizations, etc., are in possession of highly sensitive data but they want to derive meaning and patterns from the data with tools such as AI. It would be dangerous to send this private data to outside data centers hosting AI services due to the risks associated with transfer. Similarly, personal data about each individual in the form of government or tax records, or data generated from personal devices such as phones and wearables, are also private; we do not wish them to be exposed to outside parties for either training or inference. On the other hand, AI companies in possession of private models that are expensive to train might not want to reveal the weights and other details of

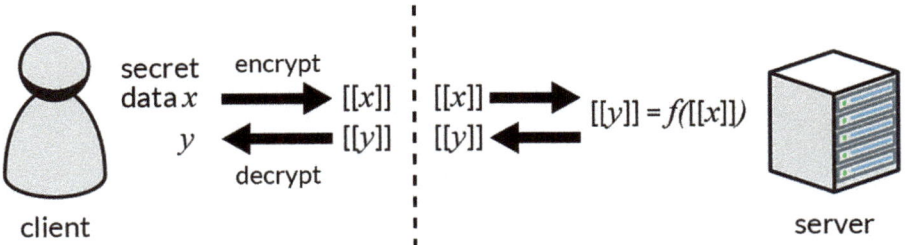

Figure 2.1. Homomorphic encryption.

their models. Hosting these models in plaintext in data centers or as a service APIs can be dangerous, as these can potentially be exploited to reveal the weights. HE solves all these problems as the secret data can stay encrypted and computation can be performed on the encrypted secret itself.

HE is often used in client-server scenarios, as illustrated in Figure 2.1. The client is in possession of encryption/decryption keys and also has secret data x. The client encrypts x to get encrypted data $[[x]]$. The encrypted data is sent to the server, which homomorphically computes a function $[[y]] = f([[x]])$ without learning anything about x. The result $[[y]]$ is sent back to the client, which decrypts it. Nothing about x or y is leaked in this process.

2.3 Hardness Assumptions

We list commonly used post-quantum hardness assumptions used in building HE schemes here. These assumptions are based on lattice cryptography as the following lattice-based problems cannot be solved easily either by classical or quantum computers.

Definition:

Let $\mathbb{R}^m$ be the m dimensional real Euclidean space. Let $\mathbf{b}_1$, $\mathbf{b}_2$, ..., $\mathbf{b}_n$ be a set of linearly independent vectors in $\mathbb{R}^m$.

A **lattice** L in $\mathbb{R}^m$ is the set of all integer linear combinations of such vectors.

$$L = \left\{ \sum_{i=1}^{n} a_i \mathbf{b}_i \,\middle|\, a_i \in \mathbb{Z} \text{ for } i = 1, 2, \ldots, n \right\}.$$

Figure 2.2a illustrates a 2D lattice with basis vectors $\mathbf{b}_1$ and $\mathbf{b}_2$. The points are in a Euclidean space and one can arrive at each point in that space by just using the basis vectors.

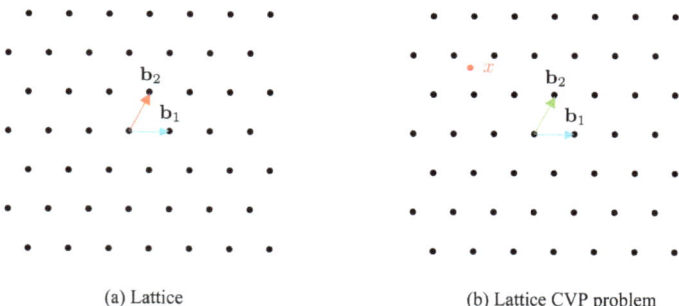

(a) Lattice   (b) Lattice CVP problem

Figure 2.2. Figure 2.2a illustrates an example of a 2D lattice with basis vectors $\mathbf{b_1}$ and $\mathbf{b_2}$. Figure 2.2b illustrates the closest vector problem. The problem is about finding a combination of the basis vectors that will lead to a lattice point that is closest to the red dot x.

Shortest Vector Problem and Closest Vector Problem:

Given a basis for the lattice and corresponding norm in a vector space, the shortest vector problem is about finding the shortest non-zero vector measured by the norm. It is equivalent to finding the closest non-zero vector to the origin. This problem is known to be average-case NP-hard to solve.

The closest vector problem is similar to shortest vector problem, except that it is about finding the vector that is closest to a specific point on the lattice. Figure 2.2b illustrates this.

Learning With Errors (LWE/RLWE)

Introduced by Regev et al. [4], LWE is about finding the secret s of N dimensions in the linear equation $A = B.s + \epsilon$, where A, and B are $(N + 1)$-dimensional vectors, and ϵ is the added error/noise. Without ϵ, s can be found in polynomial time, but with the added noise, this problem is proved to be worst-case NP-hard. RLWE (Ring LWE) extends the same concept to polynomial rings over a finite field.

2.4   Terminology

Here we define some commonly encountered terms from the HE literature.

Circuit

In cryptography, computation in some schemes is represented by Boolean circuits, and in some by arithmetic circuits. Boolean circuits can be represented as directed acyclic graphs where graph nodes are Boolean gates and graph edges indicate the flow of computation. Arithmetic circuits have similar structure and can perform computation with numbers from various algebraic structures, like field. They are commonly used to compute polynomials.

Bootstrapping

Bootstrapping is a process that refreshes the ciphertext in an FHE scheme by homomorphically decrypting the ciphertext. Note that the secret key is not used here to decrypt the ciphertext. Instead, a homomorphically encrypted secret key is used which is called the bootstrapping key to homomorphically decrypt the ciphertext.

Single Instruction, Multiple Data (SIMD)

SIMD is a parallel computing paradigm where a single computer instruction is executed on multiple elements of data at the same time. This is used to leverage data-level parallelism which shows up in operations, such as matrix multiplication. For example, in naive matrix multiplication, regardless of the size of the matrix, the operations are the same. Hence, as the size of the matrix increases, we can leverage SIMD operations to achieve more parallelism to gain speedup. SIMD is discussed in detail in 4.2.1.1.

Quantization

Quantization is a technique to reduce the precision of data types so as to reduce the memory footprint and speed up the computation. This is normally used for training and inference of neural networks in machines with low memory and low computational power. However, this can be applied to homomorphic evaluation of neural networks to reduce the high memory and compute requirements of homomorphic operations.

Residue Number System (RNS)

Homomorphic encryption schemes often use large integers which are not easily represented in computer data types. Operations like multiply need double wide types which makes the situation even worse. RNS allows us to decompose the large integers into smaller integers so that the computation can take place in native computer data types.

Number Theoretic Transform (NTT)

NTT is a generalized method for performing discrete Fourier transform (DFT) over finite fields. This often comes up in HE as NTT can be used for efficient multiplications of polynomials with integer coefficients.

2.5   Non-FHE Schemes

Even though there are many FHE schemes, it is still useful to know preceding schemes because they tend to be more efficient in terms of evaluation time or in ciphertext size and can be used in other privacy-preserving techniques such as MPC more effectively.

2.5.1   Partially Homomorphic Encryption (PHE)

PHE schemes allow evaluation of circuits with additive or multiplicative gates, depending on the scheme. Even though it appears overly limiting, PHE allows evaluation of unbounded circuit depth and is generally faster than SHE, LFHE, and FHE.

One of the most popular PHE schemes is Paillier [5], which is frequently used in privacy-preserving AI. Paillier has recently been used in Popcorn [6] to perform oblivious inference on an ImageNet [7] model, and by Ma et al. to perform a 3-party (client, data server, verification server) privacy-preserving face verification where the face features are encrypted with Paillier algorithm and verification is performed using Hamming distance [8] and oblivious transfer [9] 3.2.1 between client and verification server [10].

2.5.2   Somewhat Homomorphic Encryption (SHE)

SHE schemes allow evaluation of a subset of circuit types with multiple types of gates over arbitrary depth. Circuit types and gate types vary depending on the scheme.

2.5.3   Leveled Fully Homomorphic Encryption (LFHE)

LFHE schemes allow evaluation of arbitrary circuits with multiple types of gates of predetermined depth L. The depth depends on the parameters picked. Many FHE schemes have LFHE (and SHE) variants, as they are more efficient for the reasons discussed in the next section.

Recently, Lou et al., used Leveled Fast Homomorphic Encryption over Torus (LTFHE), which is a leveled variant of TFHE (Section 2.6.2) to achieve state-of-the-art inference accuracy on MNIST [11] and CIFAR [12] datasets at greatly reduced latency compared to previous work [13]. They implemented ResNet-18 [14], Alexnet [15], and ShuffleNet [16] for ImageNet [7], LSTM [17] for Penn Treebank [18], and ResNet-18 for CIFAR-10. No previous LFHE-enabled models could perform neural network inference of an entire ImageNet network. This is also the first LFHE-enabled model for evaluating LSTM.

2.6   FHE

FHE schemes allow evaluation of arbitrary circuits with multiple types of gates of unbounded depth. This is made possible through a process called bootstrapping.

In a (leveled) homomorphic encryption scheme, encrypting the plaintext, followed by operations such as addition and multiplication on it, results in growth of an error that becomes quite large over time. Decrypting a ciphertext with a large error results in inaccurate results and that is what prevents such a scheme from having unlimited depth. One way to completely zero out the error is to decrypt the ciphertext resulting in the plaintext. But this can introduce security vulnerabilities and can also be inefficient in a client-server environment where the client wants the server to perform some computation homomorphically on the ciphertext. Bootstrapping allows us to refresh the ciphertext by homomorphically decrypting the ciphertext.

Although a revolutionary concept, bootstrapping is known to be incredibly resource heavy. Since Gentry's seminal paper [3] introduced this bootstrapping procedure, many efficient FHE schemes have been introduced. We discuss the most popular modern FHE schemes and highlight their recent usage in AI.

2.6.1   CKKS

Homomorphic Encryption for Arithmetic of Approximate Numbers (HEAAN), which is also known as CKKS (author's last names) [19, 20], is a fourth-generation FHE scheme based on RLWE that can perform FHE on approximate arithmetic. This means that certain amounts of error during encryption, evaluation, and decryption are tolerated while still being able to decrypt the ciphertext. This is achieved by a method called rescaling that the authors introduce in the paper. CKKS also introduces a packing strategy to allow multiple messages in a single ciphertext, making it readily available for SIMD parallelism.

In CKKS, a message m consisting of n double-type complex numbers (as it supports packing) is first encoded as a polynomial t of degree $< (N - 1)$ with N integer coefficients. Then the polynomial is placed in a polynomial ring.

$$R = \mathbb{Z}[X]/(X^N + 1) \qquad (2.1)$$

The coefficients of this polynomial is in q. The polynomial t is then multiplied with a scaling factor Δ to convert it to an integer. Ciphertext $\mathbf{c}$ is obtained from this plaintext polynomial by adding it to the public key pk and some random errors e. The modulus of $\mathbf{c}$ starts with $logQ$ and as we perform multiplication, it decreases by $logp$ which is the rescaling factor. Multiplications can be performed L times, which is the number of levels or multiplicative depth after which a bootstrapping should be performed to refresh the ciphertext [21]. The parameters listed in Table 2.1 determine the security level λ of the scheme which can be calculated from equation 2.2. Security levels of HE schemes are described in 2.7.1. Note that the integers represented by the polynomials are usually too big to be represented on computers

Table 2.1. CKKS parameters.

Parameters	Description
Δ	Scaling factor
p	Rescaling factor
L	Multiplicative depth
Q	Maximum ciphertext modulus
q	Ciphertext modulus
N	Number of polynomial (of degree $N - 1$) coefficients
n	Number of messages in ciphertext, a.k.a. slots
P	Product of primes

with small word sizes (typically 64-bit). Hence, RNS is incorporated to represent the big integer as a product of integers that are pairwise coprime [22].

$$N \geq \frac{\lambda + 110}{7.2} \log(P \cdot q_L) \tag{2.2}$$

HEAAN has been used in many AI applications, including in PrivFT [23], where a GPU implementation of HEAAN was used to provide both inference as a service, and training as a service for text classification tasks such as sentiment analysis, spam detection and topic classification. Lee et al. use the RNS-variant of CKKS [22] with bootstrapping to implement the standard ResNet-20 model [14] for secure inference [24]. HEAAN has also been used to privatize BERT embeddings [25].

2.6.2 Fast Fully Homomorphic Encryption Over the Torus (TFHE)

TFHE [26] is a derivative of the FHEW scheme [27] and is known for fast Boolean gate evaluation and bootstrapping in milliseconds. Because of improvements in TFHE over the years, fixed-precision evaluations have also been possible [28]. TFHE has Torus in its name because Torus, the mathematical structure can be used to visually represent the modulo operations [29]. Just like BGV [30] and BFV [31, 32], TFHE has exact gate evaluation while evaluations in CKKS tend to be noisy. Like CKKS, TFHE is based on the LWE assumption.

A message m in TFHE is encoded into a polynomial t in the ring 2.1. The coefficients of this polynomial is in q. The ciphertext c is obtained from this plaintext polynomial by adding to the public key pk and some random errors e. This ciphertext is in GLWE which is a generalization of LWE and RLWE. RLWE is for polynomials and LWE is for individual bits. p is the plaintext modulus and the scaling factor is calculated as $\Delta = q/p$. Both p and q are powers of two.

TFHE does not support ciphertext multiplications, so the scheme uses three different ciphertext types to accomplish gate evaluations besides addition namely LWE/RLWE, RGSW [33] and GLev [28]. GLev is a generalization of Lev and RLev and it consists of a list of GLWE ciphertexts encyrpting the same message with different scaling factors Δ. Finally, GGSW (generalization of RGSW) is a list of GLev ciphertexts. TFHE defines two types of products with these ciphertexts: external product which is a product of GLWE and GGSW ciphertexts, and internal product which is a product of GGSW ciphertexts.

Since this is a leveled scheme, as more operations are performed on a ciphertext, it has to be refreshed so that the message can be recovered from the noise. For this, two types of bootstrapping are available: gate bootstrapping and circuit bootstrapping. Gate bootstrapping bootstraps the ciphertext and evaluates binary gates at the same time, and circuit bootstrapping is used for building GGSW from LWE. Programmable bootstrapping (PBS), which is a generalization of gate bootstrapping, is used to bootstrap LWE ciphertexts. Regarding the security levels of a TFHE scheme, it has to be determined using an LWE-estimator [34].

TFHE scheme has also been used for building AI applications and it is mostly suitable for tree-based machine learning models as described in Chapter 4.5. Stoian et al. perform neural network inference of networks of up to 9 layers using a library called ConcreteML [35, 36]. The library allows users to create an FHE-compatible network without any knowledge of cryptography. They provide a few standard trained models but also allow users to train their own custom models using a technique called Quantization Aware Training (QAT). Normally, neural network training and inference is done in floating points but as TFHE only supports integers, it makes sense to quantize the model so that inference can be performed easily using TFHE. In this work, instead of using post-training quantization, they use QAT as it enables extreme quantization of less than 4-bit weights and biases without losing neural network accuracy.

2.7 Standardization

HE will be used in applications such as health and medicine where patient privacy laws should be respected, and in personal technology where private information has to be kept private. Thus, it is critical that the technology provides measurable security guarantees.

HomomorphicEncryption.org has created a committee that publishes a standard for various HE schemes [37]. This committee organizes regular meetings and workshops to evaluate security and set standards for security of these schemes. Besides this organization, International Organization for Standardization (ISO) has also published a standard [38].

2.7.1 Security Level

Most of the HE schemes are based on LWE assumption. Depending on the application, users can pick parameters such as dimension, ciphertext modulus etc. The choice of these parameters dictates the security level of the scheme λ – how many operations in bits $(O(2^{\lambda}))$ it takes for known attacks to break the scheme. In the standards paper referenced above, the authors publish a table that calculates the security level for common attacks by using an LWE estimator [34].

DOI: 10.1561/9781638283454.ch3

Chapter 3

Multi-Party Computation

Multi-party computation (MPC) is a cryptographic technique where multiple parties can jointly compute a function f on their secret data, without exposing their secret data to other parties or by extension any eavesdroppers. Only the result of the computation will be revealed to all parties. In AI, MPC can be used in a multi-party setting to jointly perform training of, and inference with, neural networks on secret data.

3.1   Introduction

Formally, in an MPC scheme, a set of n participants $P = \{p_1, p_2, p_3, \ldots, p_n\}$ who each have data $D = \{d_1, d_2, d_3, \ldots, d_n\}$ can jointly compute a function $f(D)$, while keeping their respective data a secret. As illustrated in Figure 3.1, the private data of each participant d_i is never shared among other participants. Various schemes discussed in later sections are used to jointly compute $f(D)$. MPC protocols usually have an overhead of requiring a high communication cost amongst parties, and hence should be used cautiously where bandwidth and transfer limits are a concern.

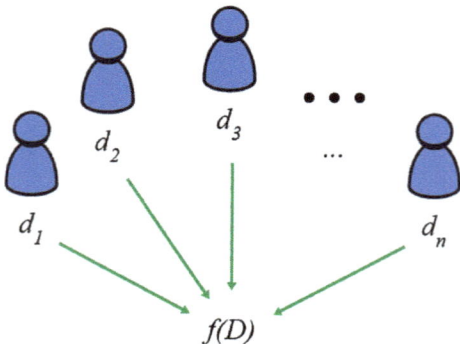

Figure 3.1. Each participant is in possession of their data d_i jointly computes $f(D)$.

In this chapter, we start by discussing various techniques that MPC schemes are based on in Section 3.2. Techniques such as garbled circuits, secret sharing, and homomorphic encryption are common approaches. We discuss various security settings that MPC schemes support in Section 3.3. Appropriate schemes can be picked depending on the MPC scenario. If an MPC protocol is adhered to by all parties, it is guaranteed that the computation will be performed correctly. However, there is a possibility of bad actors that either deviate from the protocol and do not perform their end of the computation, or try to learn about data from other parties. We discuss various threat models and approaches.

With the advent of large language models (LLMs) [39] and foundation models [40], there has been much interest in leveraging these models privately, but these models are incredibly large and computationally intensive. Hence, these models are evaluated in large data centers so that results can be availed quickly and efficiently. Unfortunately, that means that parties who want their queries to be private have to procure expensive hardware or risk leaking their inputs to these data centers. There has been work on performing fast inference on low-cost devices [41, 42] but that usually involves quantizing the models, which results in lower accuracy and still needs a capable accelerator with high memory and bandwidth requirements for fast inference. There are some MPC implementations that target inference on these foundation models. In addition, MPC has also been used in several other AI applications, and we discuss these implementations in Section 3.4.

3.2 Approaches

There are many ways to construct an MPC protocol, such as basing it on garbled circuits, secret sharing, oblivious transfer or homomorphic encryption. We next discuss each of these techniques with an illustrative example.

3.2.1 Oblivious Transfer

Oblivious transfer (OT) is a protocol between a sender and a receiver where the sender has multiple choices to offer and the receiver wants one of those choices. In this protocol, the sender does not learn about the receiver's choice, and the receiver does not learn about other choices offered by the sender. OT is heavily used in MPC protocols and supports both Boolean and arithmetic circuits.

To illustrate this, let us consider an example of 1-2 oblivious transfer with Alice and Bob (Figure 3.2).

(a) Alice holds a red-colored ball (X_{red}) and a blue-colored ball (X_{blue}) and is willing to give Bob one of them. Bob, however, does not want Alice to know which one he requested

(b) Bob sends Alice a key to encrypt X_{red} and X_{blue} in two different ways and Alice sends the encrypted results back to Bob

(c) Only one of them can be successfully decrypted. Hence, Bob only learns about the one of the two pieces of information. To Alice, the two choices for encryption are indistinguishable, so she does not learn which piece of information Bob requested.

Figure 3.2. Oblivious transfer protocol.

3.2.2   Garbled Circuit

Garbled circuits (GC) were introduced in 1986 [43] and can be used as a basis for constructing an MPC protocol. Garbling is the quintessential step in this protocol, which is where one or more parties encrypt the Boolean circuit, and then permute the input output combinations to produce a garbled circuit. This circuit can then be evaluated by parties with encrypted inputs to get an encrypted output that the garbler(s) can then share with other parties if needed.

Each computation can be decomposed into a set of Boolean functions, and each single Boolean function can be represented as a simple lookup table. The lookup table for the OR function is given in Table 3.1. The rows of the table can now be shuffled (garbled) and encrypted independently. Decrypting a single row would then reveal the truth value for a single input without revealing any other information about that function.

Consider an abstract Boolean function f with two inputs L (left input) and R (right input) that is to be computed in a secret two-party computation. One party, Alice, has four different keys – LT, LF, RT, RF – indicating that the left or the right input to be either true (T) or false (F). The output value, *True* or *False*, is then encrypted twice for each row in the table, once with one of the keys LT, LF for the first input and a second time with one of the keys RT, RF. This gives four encrypted values ($E(LTRT), E(LTRF), E(LFRT), E(LFRF)$), each of which can only be decrypted with a different combination of the four keys. The unordered list of the four encrypted values is then sent to Bob. Bob can ask Alice for two keys: one from LT, LF and one from RT, RF. He tries to decode all four encrypted values but will only be successful for one of them. This will be the value of the Boolean function he wants to compute. If Alice and Bob use OT in the last step, where Bob requests one of the 2 keys LT, LF and one of RT, RF, Alice does not learn anything about the function value Bob computed, and Bob does not learn anything about the function, except the specific function value of his input.

We illustrate this exchange with Figure 3.3 which shows a two-party MPC protocol based on Yao's garbled circuit. Yao's garbled circuit can be used to solve Yao's millionaire problem: Two millionaires want to know which one of them is richer

Table 3.1. Truth table for OR operation.

Input 1	Input 2	Output
False	False	False
False	True	True
True	False	True
True	True	True

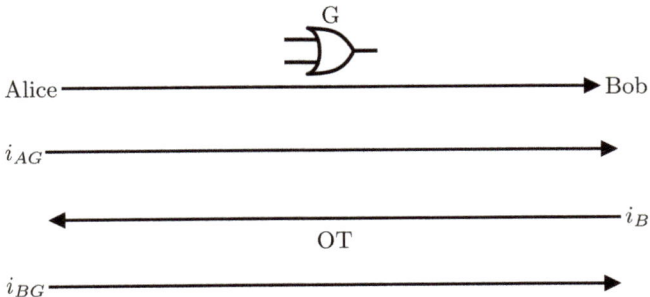

Figure 3.3. Describes a simple two-party MPC protocol with garbled circuit.

without revealing their net worth to each other. This protocol can also be used to perform two-party computation on any Boolean circuit. In the figure, we have an OR gate as an example. Alice and Bob know the gate beforehand and can perform an OR operation. Alice's input is i_A and Bob's input is i_B, at the end of this protocol, both want to know the result $o = i_A \lor i_B$ without either party learning about other party's input.

To accomplish this, Alice first garbles the circuit (encryption, permutation) and her garbled input $i_A -> i_{AG}$ and sends both of them over to Bob. Bob needs his input garbled so that he can perform $o_G = i_{AG} \lor i_{BG}$. he sends i_B via OT. OT guarantees that Alice does not learn about Bob's ungarbled input and is discussed below. Alice sends garbled input $i_B G$ to Bob. Bob finally evaluates circuit and sends the result over to Alice. Alice can now decrypt the answer and can share it with Bob if needed.

One drawback of GC is that the circuits are not reusable for new inputs without compromising security and thus the circuits have to be regarbled every time inputs change.

3.2.3   Secret Sharing

With secret sharing, a secret s can be split into n shares in such a way that $t \leq n$ (threshold) shares can reveal the secret. This can be accomplished in many ways. Most MPC protocols use additive secret sharing or Shamir's secret sharing (which is also additive) [44]. For protocols that support multiplication, usually, Beaver triples [45], OT, or homomorphic encryption are used instead. A drawback of secret sharing is that each share should be at least as long as the secret.

Additive Secret Sharing

In an additive secret-sharing scheme defined over a finite field (e.g. $\mathbb{Z}_p$ which is an integer modulo of prime p), the secret s is split into n shares and each of the n parties holds on to their share. For illustration, we pick a scheme where n shares are

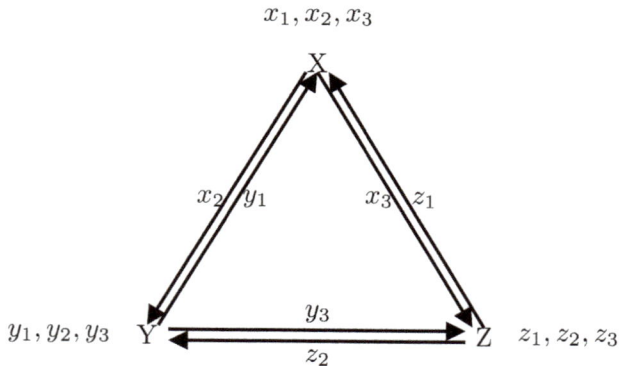

Figure 3.4. Secret sharing with three parties X, Y, and Z.

needed to arrive at the secret. Although, an $n - 1$ additive secret sharing scheme can also be constructed.

Figure 3.4 illustrates a simple additive scheme where parties X, Y, and Z exchange their shares $x = \sum_{i=1}^{3} x_i, y = \sum_{i=1}^{3} y_i$, and $z = \sum_{i=1}^{3} z_i$ respectively. At the end of the exchange, each party computes the partial sums, e.g., X computes $S_x = x_1 + y_1 + z_1$ and then shares the partial sums freely with other parties. Finally, after the exchange of partial sums, each party has S_x, S_y, and S_z and when added up, it reveals the secret $S = S_x + S_y + S_z = \sum_{i=1}^{3} x_i + \sum_{i=1}^{3} y_i + \sum_{i=1}^{3} z_i = x + y + z$.

Shamir's Secret Sharing

Shamir's secret sharing (SSS) is another additive secret sharing scheme that is defined using polynomials over a finite field. Unlike the additive scheme discussed above, SSS can be defined for any threshold $t \leq n$. Only t shares are needed to reveal the secret. This works because SSS takes advantage of polynomial interpolation: t points are sufficient to come up with a unique polynomial curve of degree $\leq t - 1$. If only $t - 1$ shares (points) are given, there are infinitely many possible polynomials that can pass through those points. Another advantage of SSS is that the scheme is information-theoretically secure 3.3.1.

Beaver Triples

Beaver triples are three numbers a, b, and c, which are secret shared among participants. Once the participants get the secret shared triples, they jointly compute $x - a$ and $y - b$, which are then publicly revealed. Then, each participant i computes $z_i = c_i + (x - a)b_i + (y - b)a_i$. Subsequently, the participants add the product of public value $(x - a)(y - b)$ to the secret-shared z_i, and then all participants open z to reveal the product xy. This works because of an interesting property: $\sum_i z_i = c + (x - a)b + (y - b)a + (x - a)(y - b) = xy$. The Beaver triples cannot be used for another multiplication without revealing information about the secrets we are trying to multiply, so new triples have to be generated for each new multiplication.

3.2.4 Homomorphic Encryption

MPC is more commonly based on secret sharing and garbled circuit, but it can also be based on HE, discussed in detail in the previous chapter. In the following sections, we discuss MPC protocols that use various HE schemes, such as SHE and FHE.

3.3 Security Settings

This section discusses various security scenarios that arise in the discussion of the underlying machinery of MPC. An appropriate protocol must be chosen depending on the type of adversaries in the system.

3.3.1 Information-Theoretic Security

A protocol is said to be information-theoretically (IT) secure if it is secure against adversaries that have unlimited compute power and time. This also means that if a protocol is IT secure, it is quantum-resistant. The probability of breaking the cryptosystem by an adversary would be minuscule in IT secure protocols. A protocol is said to have *perfect security* if it has zero probability of an adversary with unlimited compute power and time breaking the system.

3.3.2 Semi-honest Security

If a cryptosystem has semi-honest security, that means that the system is secure against honest-but-curious adversaries – the parties do not deviate from the protocol but might be curious about the keys and random numbers that are given to them by other parties, and might try to make sense of it. This system is not secure against malicious adversaries – parties that can deviate from the protocol, eavesdrop, or collect data.

On the same note, there are protocols that are honest majority, which means that it is secure against situations where there are $(n-1)$ honest parties out of n.

3.3.3 Active Security

A cryptosystem that has active security is secure against malicious adversaries. A dishonest majority protocol is one that is secure even if malicious adversaries are in the majority (e.g. all but one are dishonest). There can also be protocols that offer security midway between semi-honest and active security, such as against covert adversaries – where adversaries might try to go against the protocol but do not want to risk getting caught. Protocols that are secure against covert adversaries may assign a probability of cheat detection.

3.4   MPC Protocols Used in AI

MPC protocols such as SPDZ, MASCOT, and others are being used in AI not only because of the features of the protocol but also because of the availability of libraries that are built specifically for AI tasks.

3.4.1   SPDZ

SPDZ [46–48] and its variants have gained adoption in privacy-preserving AI applications in the last few years. The original SPDZ and SPDZ-2 [47] protocols are based on additive secret sharing and Beaver triples. Depending on the application, the protocol can be used for one of honest-but-curious (semi-honest), covert, or malicious security (dishonest majority or active security) assumptions.

Most of the communication overhead in evaluating a circuit with SPDZ comes from secure generation and secret sharing of triples. SPDZ optimizes this process by splitting the protocol into an offline (pre-processing) phase and an online phase. Since generation of multiplication triples is independent of the circuit to be evaluated, the triples can be generated in the offline phase and the circuit is evaluated in the online phase. In the original SPDZ paper [46], each party uses SHE described in Chapter 2.5.2 to generate the triples. The values generated in the offline phase can only be used for evaluating one function here. For subsequent functions, offline phase has to be repeated from scratch. In the subsequent paper [47], there is no such limitation. Furthermore, most of the computation is offloaded to the offline phase resulting in a faster online phase.

CrypTen [49] is a PyTorch-based [50] MPC framework for machine learning applications and uses a semi-honest security version of SPDZ under the hood. It offers popular machine learning abstractions that are common in modern machine learning frameworks to make it easy for developers to leverage MPC in their machine learning training or inference of their models. In addition to tensor computation, neural network model abstraction, optimizers, automatic differentiation, it also offers GPU support for faster training/inference. Another assumption that the library makes is that there is a trusted third party that generates Beaver triples. Although it does support arbitrary number of parties. They also provide benchmarks and samples for machine learning tasks, such as text classification, speech recognition, and image classification.

CrypTen has been used by Adams et al. for private text classification without exposing the text of the data owner or exposing the model parameters of the model owner's classification model [51]. In a two-party setting of text-owner and model-owner, the authors reveal that the scheme can securely classify customer review texts in 0.74s in sequential mode and in 0.11s in batch mode.

3.4.2   MP-SPDZ and MASCOT

MASCOT [52] is an MPC protocol that improves on SPDZ's (active security) runtime by 200x by using OT to perform secure multiplications with reduced communication and computation, and exploits parallelism with use of SSE [53] instructions. MASCOT improves SPDZ in the offline phase, where it uses OT to speed up the triple generation, while still offering active security. MP-SPDZ (Multi-Protocol SPDZ) [54, 55] is an open-source implementation of 34 MPC protocol variants of SPDZ-2 (includes MASCOT) by the authors and it presents a high-level programming interface based on Python. MP-SPDZ also offers functions for machine learning applications like regression, decision trees, SGD and Adam optimizers, layers like dense, convolution, maxpool and dropout, along with functionality for loading of pre-trained models.

3.4.3   Two-Party, Three-Party, and Four-Party Computation

In some cases, there might not be a need for protocols that generalize to arbitrary number of parties in the protocol. There might be instances like peer-to-peer networks where only a handful of parties are trying to jointly compute a function. Hence there are protocols designed where there are only 2 parties (2PC), 3 parties (3PC), 4 parties (4PC), etc. Some of these protocols use m-out-of-n secret sharing which means that m secret shares are sufficient to reconstruct the secret.

There are several 2PC, 3PC, and 4PC protocols such as Cheetah [56] which is a 2PC based on secret sharing, homomorphic encryption and OT for the inference of deep neural networks in a semi-honest setting. ABY3 [57] which is a 3PC protocol with semi-honest assumption designed for machine learning applications, and Fantastic Four [58] which is a 4PC secret sharing based protocol providing malicious security. Some of the recent applications of these protocols in AI applications are highlighted below.

CryptGPU [59] is a GPU-accelerated MPC library described in Chapter 4.7.1 that implements 2-out-of-3 replicated secret sharing (3PC) in a honest-majority setting that fully accelerated MPC protocols on the GPU and is based on CrypTen.

Chatbots based on LLMs increasingly see private information in queries. PUMA [60] aims to bring privacy-preserving AI to LLMs [39]: specifically inference on Llama-7B [61]. This is a great step forward in private prompting on LLMs. PUMA implements a transformer layer and high quality efficient approximations for non-linear functions such as GeLU and softmax. The authors claim the method to be about two times faster than MPCFormer [62] and that it can evaluate Llama-7B in 5 minutes to generate 1 token. This is still quite slow compared to plaintext but is a step in the right direction towards private LLM inference.

Part II

Acceleration

DOI: 10.1561/9781638283454.ch4

Chapter 4

Accelerating Homomorphic Encryption and Multi-Party Computation

Homomorphic encryption (HE) and multi-party computation (MPC) protocols can be slow in practice. However, they can be accelerated by various accelerators such as multi-core CPUs, GPUs (Graphics Processing Units), FPGAs (Field-Programmable Gate Arrays), and ASICs (Application-Specific Integrated Circuits) to make them practical for artificial intelligence (AI) applications. We discuss the bottlenecks in these protocols and various ways of mitigating them. We then discuss recent works that mitigate bottlenecks with accelerators and enable use in AI applications.

4.1 Introduction

For privacy-preserving AI to be ubiquitous, it needs to be accelerated by a large magnitude. Luckily, there has been much progress in hardware technologies allowing for higher performance in matrix operations, which are used extensively in cryptographic protocols and in AI. Faster and more efficient caching allow for acceleration of HE schemes which tend to be memory bandwidth bound. Furthermore, there have been advances in special-purpose chips such as FPGAs and ASICs that allow for acceleration of routines that cannot be easily parallelized by off-the-shelf hardware accelerators. In addition to accelerating compute, these chips can also accelerate networking operations, which are crucial for the acceleration of MPC schemes.

This chapter starts with a description of widely used accelerators for AI and privacy-preserving techniques in Section 4.2. There are general purpose accelerators available such as multi-core CPUs and SoCs and there are special purpose accelerators such as GPUs, FPGAs, and ASICs that are designed to be incredibly fast at performing certain bottleneck tasks. Section 4.3 discusses essential functions that are ripe for acceleration to gain speedup in HE. Techniques and recent work on accelerating HE schemes are discussed in Section 4.4 and 4.5. Two popular homomorphic schemes, CKKS and Fast Fully Homomorphic Encryption over the Torus (TFHE), are compared in Section 4.6. Finally, Section 4.7 discusses the acceleration of MPC schemes.

4.2   Accelerators

Accelerators are special purpose devices that can be used to accelerate components of a computation. For example, if a part of the computation can be performed in SIMD (Single Instruction, Multiple Data), vector instructions like AVX-512 [63] can be used on certain CPUs to execute one operation, such as addition on sixteen 32-bit floats (512-bit data) at the same time.

4.2.1   Multi-Core CPU

Moore's Law [64] is a historically accurate trend that the number of transistors will double in new chips every two years. Traditionally, chip makers relied on making the transistors smaller and adding more transistors to increase the density, but this trajectory is reaching the limits of physical possibility. As a way to resolve this, more compute units (or cores) were introduced in each processor to achieve parallelism. In addition, SIMD and vector instructions were introduced.

4.2.1.1   SIMD

SIMD instructions can be used to execute a single instruction on a wide bit, such as 128, 256, or even a 512-bit input. These instructions are accompanied by registers that are as wide. During execution, multiple smaller bits can be packed into one wide bit so that they can be computed in parallel. Figure 4.1 illustrates a SIMD processing unit with an instruction cache that issues one instruction at a time that each of the eight 32-bit floating point units executes in parallel. Inputs are loaded from either registers or memory.

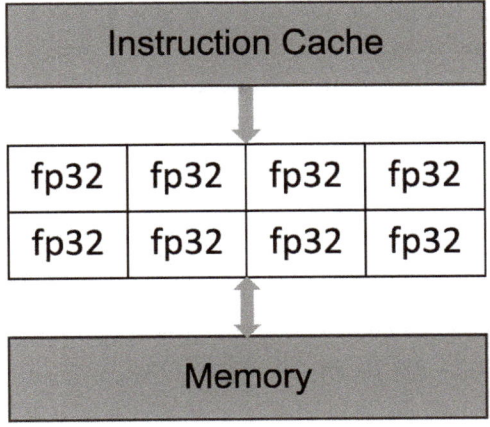

Figure 4.1. Architecture of a SIMD processing unit.

SIMD instruction sets for the x86 architecture include SSE, AVX, and Fused Multiply Add (FMA). For example, the FMA instruction $VFMADD231PD$ [63] $ymm1, ymm2, ymm3/m256$ can perform the operation,

$$ymm1 = ymm2 * ymm3/m256 + ymm1 \tag{4.1}$$

where $ymm1$, $ymm2$, and $ymm3$ refer to AVX registers that are 256-bit wide. $ymm3/m256$ indicates that this operand can either be a YMM register or a 256-bit memory address. This operation happens on packed double precision floating point values (PD).

SIMD and vector instructions can be used to achieve parallelism at a lower level in the programming stack. For most applications and optimizations, programmers can just leverage compilers to generate these instructions from their code.

4.2.1.2 Multi-core and Threading

Multi-core and threading on the other hand can facilitate task and data parallelism at a higher level with less effort. Programming languages and libraries like OpenMP [65], C++17 [66], and Rayon for Rust [67, 68] can be used to parallelize any part of the code that can leverage task and data parallelism at thread-level.

4.2.2 GPUs

GPUs were originally designed to process graphics workloads. Graphics processing involves processing large 2D or 3D arrays and displaying them on the screen at high frame rates. GPUs have evolved a lot over the years and have been used for general-purpose tasks and they are incidentally called GPGPU (General-purpose computing on GPU). Because it was used to originally solve the problem of rendering large multi-dimensional arrays, they can achieve massive parallelism. Unlike CPUs, a single GPU can launch up to hundreds to thousands of threads that can run in parallel at a time. Programs that run on the GPU are called kernels.

Certain mathematical operations can take advantage of this massive parallelism, processing large amounts of data quickly. As a result GPUs have revolutionized the field of AI. Neural network training and inference mostly involves matrix operation for which standard open-source and vendor-provided libraries exist and can be drop-in replaced to quickly accelerate the task. Training that can take days on multi-core CPUs can be performed in hours on a GPU. Similarly, cryptographic schemes can also leverage this parallelism for significant speedups.

4.2.2.1 Architecture

NVIDIA, Intel, and AMD are major GPU vendors, with most AI applications using NVIDIA GPUs. Although there are significant differences in microarchitecures of each GPU, Figure 4.2 seeks to illustrate the essential elements with a generic architecture for a PCIe [69] connected GPU. Each GPU has a VRAM (Video Random Access Memory) or HBM (High Bandwidth Memory) of its own that is then connected to the computer (processor) via PCIe. The memory is cached via L2 and is shared among multiple SMs (Steaming Multiprocessors/Compute Units). Each SM has GPU cores, which are SIMD processing units. Some manufacturers, like AMD, sometimes use VLIW (Very Long Instruction Word) instead. Each of these GPU cores can process fp32 (32-bit floating point) in SIMD fashion. MAC (Multiply Accumulate) is another unit that is used for faster matrix operations

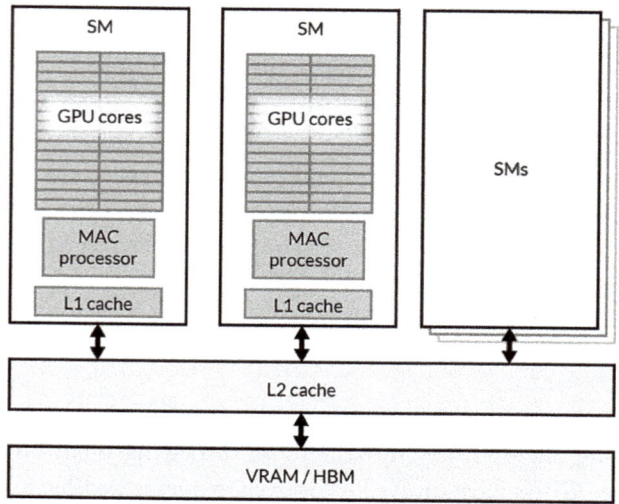

Figure 4.2. Architecture of PCIe GPUs.

Table 4.1. Comparison of different data formats.

Format	Description
FP8	8-bit floating point. A compact representation of floating-point numbers, offering less precision and range than FP16 or FP32.
FP16	16-bit floating point (half precision). 5-bit exponent and 10-bit fraction
FP32	32-bit floating point (single precision). 8-bit exponent and 23-bit fraction
FP64	64-bit floating point (double precision). 11-bit exponent and 52-bit fraction
BF16	Bfloat16 (brain floating point). 8-bit exponent and 7-bit fraction. With more bits for exponent than fp16, bf16 can have as much numeric range as fp32.
INT8	8-bit integer. Used in quantized neural networks for edge devices and LLMs [39]

explained in more detail below. Each SM also has an L1 cache which can be shared among the GPU cores and MAC.

NVIDIA GPUs

NVIDIA calls their GPGPU architecture CUDA (Compute Unified Device Architecture) which is also the name for their API and programming language (CUDA C/C++).

Each NVIDIA GPU consists of several Streaming Multiprocessors (SMs), each of which have multiple CUDA cores. Each CUDA core can launch a group of 32 threads, which are collectively called a *warp*. To execute a warp efficiently, only one instruction should be issued to it. The H100 GPU in PCIe form has 114 SMs [70], each of which has 128 fp32 CUDA cores. Each SM also has 4 tensor cores. Tensor cores are special cores that can perform faster MACs($D = A * B + C$) than using CUDA cores. Tensor cores also allow for smaller types such as fp8, fp16, bf16, and int8 (Table 4.1) which are useful for faster, but less precise, computation. This is useful in performing training and inference of large models on a GPU with smaller VRAMs. Several SMs also share one or two L2 caches and each SM has an L1 cache, which is also called shared memory.

AMD GPUs

AMD calls their GPGPU architecture CDNA (Compute DNA) and their GPU architecture RDNA (Radeon DNA). These GPUs are programmed using either HIP (C++ Heterogeneous-Compute Interface for Portability), which is part of the ROCm stack (Radeon Open Compute meta-project) [71], or OpenCL [72].

Similar to NVIDIA GPUs, each CDNA3 GPU has multiple CUs (Compute Units), each of which have several shader cores and a few matrix cores. Each CU can launch a group of 64 threads, called a wavefront. The MI300X accelerator, which is equivalent to the H100, has 304 CUs [73, 74], each with 4x 16-wide SIMD shader cores and 4x matrix cores that are specially designed for AI for matrix operations and also support the above special data types. The CUs share an L2 cache, and each CU has an L1 cache called local data share (LDS) which is analogous to shared memory in NVIDIA architectures.

4.2.3   TPUs

Tensor Processing Units (TPUs) are ASICs optimized for training and inference of large AI models [75] by Google. While mostly used for accelerating AI applications, they are also used to accelerate cryptographic protocols and operations [76]. TPUs are organized into pods and each pod has hundreds to thousands of chips connected by high-bandwidth interfaces. Each chip has one or two TensorCores [77] that consist of matrix multiply units that can perform an 128x128 matrix multiply-accumulate (MAC), vector units, and a scalar unit. The multiply in the MAC operation takes bfloat16 inputs and the accumulate is performed in fp32. Vector units are used for activation functions such as rectified linear unit (ReLU) or softmax. The scalar unit is used for control flow and maintenance operations. TPUs are mostly isolated to data centers and are not as widely available as GPUs.

4.2.4   FPGAs

Field-Programmable Gate Arrays (FPGAs) are special integrated circuits that can be reprogrammed. Like ASICs, they can be designed for a specific purpose, but can also be reprogrammed to iterate on the circuit design. Configurable Logic Blocks (CLB) are the building blocks of an FPGA as each of these can be configured to build any kind of circuit. FPGAs are useful for prototyping, as well as for deployment, and have been used for developing chips for accelerating parts of cryptographic, mathematical, or other computations that can be accelerated with a specialized circuit.

Even though accelerators like GPUs are much more prevalent, they are not as capable as FPGAs for accelerating most parts of HE and MPC computations in AI as they are mostly used to speed up multiplications and some of the more complex operations like FFT. The advantage of accelerating with FPGA is that highly specialized operations can be programmed-in right on the hardware for acceleration.

Besides accelerating multiplications, FPGAs can also be used to implement SmartNICs [78], which can be used in distributed cryptographic protocols like MPC, which tend to have very high network cost compared to compute cost.

4.2.5   Performance Measures

Performance of an HPC system/accelerator can be categorized into peak compute performance and peak bandwidth availability.

Table 4.2. Bandwidth capabilities.

Component	Bandwidth
Caches (L1, L2, L3)	TB/s
GPU Memory (VRAM/HBM)	TB/s
SXM 5	Up to TB/s
GPU interconnects (NVLINK/die stacking)	GB/s to TB/s
PCIe 5.0	Up to 128 GB/s
Network Interconnects (Data centers)	Hundreds of GB/s
Network Interconnects (Outside Data centers)	Varies

Compute performance is measured with FLOPS (floating operations per second) which measures the amount of floating point operations the system can perform in one second. A single accelerator like NVIDIA H100 PCIe can do a peak of 756 teraFLOPS of fp32 tensor operations, which are used for neural network related tasks, and a peak of 51 teraFLOPS of fp32 for HPC applications [79].

Memory bandwidth is another measurement that is used to ensure that the application can load the data into registers before executing instructions. This is measured in MB/s, GB/s, TB/s, etc. Table 4.2 lists the bandwidth of various components.

But the peak performance measures are not always reachable because of many reasons such as the type of problem being solved which can be compute-bound or memory-bound, algorithm design, compiler optimizations and design, and program designs. The units throughput and latency are used instead to measure realistic performance.

4.3   Essential Functions in HE

We discuss the functions that are essential to HE. These functions show up quite frequently and accelerating them will result in impactful speedup.

4.3.1   Polynomial Multiplication and Number Theoretic Transform

Component-wise polynomial additions and multiplications are just modular additions and multiplications and can be performed in $\mathcal{O}(N)$. Polynomial multiplications on the other hand are more resource intensive as the result of the multiplication is a convolution of the input polynomials. Naively it can be performed in $\mathcal{O}(N^2)$ but with Number Theoretic Transform (NTT) [80], it can be done in $\mathcal{O}(NlogN)$. NTT is like FFT but operates on modular arithmetic.

NTT has become one of the fundamental techniques used to optimize polynomial multiplications.

4.3.2 Key-switching

Key switching is an operation that allows one to move from one ciphertext modulus Q to another Q'. This is necessary because operations like multiplication effectively double the modulus of the results, and to perform further computation with this result we need to switch the modulus. Key switching is considered one of the biggest bottlenecks in FHE systems and involves performing several NTTs, additions, and multiplications, which are themselves heavy operations. Most acceleration efforts are devoted to improving the efficiency of this operation and making sure that it accesses memory with reduced cache hits.

4.4 Accelerating CKKS

CKKS and similar lattice-based schemes can be accelerated at various layers of the software and hardware stack. On the hardware stack, optimizations can be done on commodity hardware, and accelerators can be used in tandem to achieve higher circuit evaluation throughput. Alternatively, specialized hardware such as FPGAs and ASICs can be used to achieve maximum throughput. On the software stack, improvements can be made through parallelization and code optimizations that use hardware intrinsics, optimal memory accesses, algorithmic optimizations, and changes in cryptographic techniques.

Most of the work has been done on the server-side of HE because that is where most of the processing is done. Encryption and decryption happens on the client-side and it is usually on small amounts of data.

4.4.1 Bottlenecks

First, Castro et al. observed that in FHE implementations, bootstrapping exhibits a low arithmetic intensity of < 1 operation/byte as a consequence of it being heavily main memory bandwidth bound [81]. They also pointed out that improvements in arithmetic throughput by using special arithmetic hardware has resulted in marginal gains and that significant gains can be achieved by bridging the memory bandwidth gap. The paper also mentions that for parameters that render 128-bits of security (which is considered secure), the ciphertext size blows up to $\sim$73.4 MB, which is too large for cache sizes of CPUs. Note that there have been improvements in cache sizes since then and the largest available cache size per chip is 1152MB in AMD EPYC™ 9684X CPU. 9684X has 12 CCDs (complex core dies) each with 32MB L3 cache with an additional 64MB 3D V-cache. Since the paper increases utilization of cache even with smaller L3 cache sizes of just 32MB per CCD, it would be interesting to see the results on CPUs with bigger L3 caches sizes.

Similar conclusions were drawn in F1 [82], where authors find that the movement of homomorphically encrypted data, which typically is at least 50 times larger than plaintext, and auxiliary data poses the key challenge in FHE acceleration. They also point to key-switching, which is an essential part of homomorphic multiplication as the most expensive operation. Since on-chip storage and memory bandwidth is limited, optimizations must be made in such operations to get the most out of what is available. This work claims that the F1 accelerator, an ASIC, is the first programmable accelerator and can enable real-time fully homomorphic deep learning inference in the cloud. F1 also supports other CKKS-like schemes such as BGV [30] and GSW [33]. Some of the drawbacks of F1 is that it does not support packed bootstrapping (multi-slot), and it only supports slot sizes up to $N = 16K$.

4.4.2   FPGA and ASIC

Besides the papers described above, there have been several solutions to accelerate CKKS-like FHE schemes on FPGA and ASICs that have resulted in a phenomenal increase in performance.

The follow-up paper from Castro et al., implements CKKS on a standard commercially available multi-FPGA system that outperforms all prior FPGA implementations and outperforms the CPU by 456x, the GPU by 6.5x, and F1 by 12x for training logistic regression [83]. ARK [84] is an ASIC FHE accelerator that improves upon prior works like F1, and improves the parameter requirements for efficient and practical bootstrapping. ARK can perform real-time convolutional neural network inference on the ResNet-20 model in 0.125 seconds. REED [85] introduces the first chiplet architecture for accelerating FHE with 2.5D packaging technology. To solve the computation-communication bottleneck, they introduce an inter-chiplet communications strategy that ensures computation-communication parallelism. This chip can supposedly train an MNIST neural network with two hidden layers and one output layer for ~7000 iterations with ~5.8 bootstrappings per iteration that achieves 95.2% accuracy in 7.7 minutes. The same using OpenFHE [86] on 24-core, 2×Intel Xeon CPU X5690 @ 3.47GHz takes 29 days. Chiplet approaches are more scalable than one-off designs and can also be made much more efficient in terms of power consumption.

4.4.3   GPU

A paper [87] often dubbed "100x" accelerates multiple essential functions of CKKS including bootstrapping. They apply optimizations like kernel fusion where multiple GPU kernels are merged into one to reduce the number of memory accesses between kernels and thus going around the memory bandwidth bottlenecks. For training of logistic regression models, they report a 40x speedup over multi-core CPU.

TensorFHE is a fast GPU-accelerated implementation of FHE [88]. It boosts the GPGPU implementation of CKKS by up to 2.61x compared to previous state-of-the-art described above. They analyze NTT at a microarchitecture level and improve its performance by replacing the butterfly algorithm with matrix-vector multiplication, they further utilize tensor cores available in newer NVIDIA architectures for NTT. They also fully utilize data parallelism through operation-level batching.

Going back to the architecture of GPUs described in previous sections, we can see that each CUs/SMs have a local shared memory and any memory transfers between them is expensive as it needs to go through the L2 cache. This is not great for FHE functions because they have wide vectors that cannot fit into one CU. GME [89] explores what would happen if CUs can efficiently communicate with each other. They also propose several GPU microarchitectural enhancements, scheduler, and a simulator infrastructure called Blocksim for investigating GPU architecture that is suitable for FHE. All of these proposed optimizations are applied to AMD CDNA architecture and are implemented on a cycle-accurate GPU architecture simulator called NaviSim [90]. With these proposed changes, secure inference can be performed on ResNet-20 in 982ms, and logistic regression can be performed in 54.5ms which is 2.9x faster than 100x [87].

Recently, GPU implementation of CKKS was applied to privatize Bidirectional Encoder Representations from Transformers (BERT) embeddings [91]. BERT is a neural network commonly used for training large language models [39] and it is based on transformers [40] architecture which revolutionized the field of AI recently. Embedding layer compresses the input of a neural network into semantics-preserving low-dimensional vector which is then fed to downstream text classification tasks. However, embeddings can still leak data of the text it was trained on. Lee et al. homomorphically encrypt the pre-trained embeddings of BERT and then build a homomorphic logistic regression-based classifier with GPU-accelerated CKKS [91]. The trained model can then be used for downstream tasks with minimal loss in accuracy.

4.5　Accelerating TFHE

TFHE is known for its fast bootstrapping speed and programmable bootstrapping (PBS), which not only refreshes the ciphertext but also lets us evaluate arbitrary univariate functions that can be represented by lookup tables [92]. Unlike CKKS, TFHE doesn't inherently support packing of ciphertexts, which makes acceleration on data-parallel accelerators challenging. However, because of fast programmable bootstrapping, TFHE can run quite fast on CPUs.

4.5.1 CPU

On CPU, Concrete and ConcreteML [36, 93] provide the most extensive support for utilizing TFHE for AI applications. ConcreteML offers some built-in models that are best suited for TFHE schemes such as linear regression, decision trees [94], XGBoost [95] and random forest [96], as well as deep neural network models with QAT (Quantization-Aware Training) for MNIST, CIFAR10 and CIFAR100, and for evaluation of one layer of the GPT-2 [97] LLM [39, 98].

4.5.2 FPGA and ASICs

Strix [99] is an ASIC made for evaluating TFHE over streaming data at high throughput. They achieve over 1067x higher throughput compared to CPU implementation (Concrete), 37x higher throughput over the GPU implementation [100], and 7.4x over the state-of-the-art ASIC called Matcha [101], which was the first ASIC designed for TFHE. In Strix, authors identify that blind rotation operation during the PBS step runs sequentially, leading to significant performance degradation. They incorporate device-level and core-level batching using specialized hardware units and thus exploit parallellism and amortize the cost of blind rotation.

They benchmark their performance for MNIST inference on neural network NN-20, NN-50, and NN-100. NN-20 for example has an input layer with 10x11 convolution, followed by ReLU activation. Next i ($i = 20, 50, 100$) layers each have 92 neurons [102] followed by ReLU. ReLU is performed during PBS. For comparison, they use Concrete library with Intel Xeon Platinum CPU (details not specified) running Concrete, and NVIDIA Titan RTX GPU running nuFHE. They report 33-38x gains over the CPU and 8-17x gains over the GPU.

4.5.3 GPU

There are three main implementations of TFHE on the GPU with comparable performance metrics for FFT and NTT: cuFHE [103], nuFHE [100], and Concrete-cuda [104]. nuFHE and cuFHE accelerate the NTT/FFT part of the bootstrapping algorithm, and Concrete-cuda accelerates PBS and key switching. The latter offers two types of bootstrapping depending on the workload. Low latency bootstrap is used for < 10 simultaneous bootstraps and amortized bootstrap is for accelerating > 10 bootstraps.

Table 4.3. Comparison of CKKS and TFHE HE Schemes.

Feature	CKKS	TFHE
Bootstrapping speed	Seconds to minutes [87]	Milliseconds to seconds [27]
Scheme type	Approximate arithmetic	Exact
Ciphertext	Packed	No packing
Input format	Complex, integer	Boolean, integer, fixed-precision
Bottleneck	Memory bound	Throughput
Best suited for	Neural networks	General AI, decision trees, random forest
Polynomial multiplications	NTT	FFT/NTT

4.6   Comparing CKKS and TFHE

The Table 4.3 lists the differences between CKKS and TFHE for high performance privacy-preserving AI.

4.7   Accelerating MPC

High performance MPC protocols in AI are mostly accelerated through the use of GPUs. Since HE takes place across two parties with asymmetric capabilities, it is sufficient for the HE server to have an expensive, high performing processor or co-processor. But in the case of MPC, the capabilities of all parties should be more or less equal. There are protocols where a trusted party with high performance compute does some of the compute/memory intensive parts of the computation for the rest of the parties, but this is not secure.

Another thing to note is that MPC protocols tend to be communication-intensive, so adding more compute-based solutions to solve this problem might not be helpful after a certain point. In some cases, acceleration can be achieved by reducing the communication required or by using network optimizers/accelerators. We discuss the latest efforts to accelerate MPC protocols here.

4.7.1   GPU Accelerated MPC

CrypTen [49], which was discussed in Chapter 3.4.1, offers a machine learning focused API in PyTorch and natively supports running functions on the GPU. One challenge in performing SPDZ on the GPU is that integer computations are not supported on the GPUs. To solve this problem, CrypTen decomposes the 64-bit integer a into four components $a = a_0 + 2^{16}a_1 + 2^{32}a_2 + 2^{48}a_3$ and then performs computations like convolutions and products by multiplying the 16-bit a_i pairwise (with b_i for instance) on the GPU using optimized floating-point CUDA kernels. They find that CrypTen is 1–2 magnitudes faster on GPUs (NVIDIA Tesla P100) than on CPUs (Intel Skylake 18-core 1.6GHz). On that setup, CrypTen takes 8.47s to perform two-party inference on the ViT-B/16 [105] model, which is a vision transformer model that has 12 multi-head self-attention layers [106] with 12 heads each. It takes ~0.3 GB of communication between parties to achieve that.

CryptGPU [59] is a library that is based on CrypTen but only considers MPC in a three party setting (3PC) and uses replicated 2-out-of-3 secret sharing instead of Beaver triples. It is secure against a single semi-honest party.

4.7.2   FPGA/ASIC Accelerated MPC

PPMLAC [107] introduces two FPGA prototypes, one as an ASIC and another as a protoype for a RISC-V [108] CPU with extended instructions for MPC. This chip is able to run maliciously secure secret sharing MPC and is capable of running large-scale complex machine learning models like ResNet-18 [14] at high performance. Mainly, PPMLAC focuses on reducing communication between the parties by a) locally generating pseudo random numbers (trusted chip) instead of jointly generating Beaver triples b) re-using secrets using a secure secret cache c) synchronization of the chips through one-way communication to remove bottlenecks. In a Trans-Pacific two-party setting with 200ms round-trip latency, they find that PPMLAC achieves 280x speedup over semi-honest secure CrypTen running on NVIDIA Tesla V100 GPU and 300000× speedup over maliciously secure MP-SPDZ. Two-party Resnet-18 inference with the 200ms network latency runs in less than 4s.

Patel et al. introduce FPGA-based smartNIC along with an MPC accelerator that can saturate a 100Gb/s link available through COPA (Intel's Configurable Network Protocol Accelerator) [109, 110]. COPA enables remote accelerator triggering between MPC participants, which reduces the need for explicit synchronize commands. For the MPC, they use the Fantastic Four protocol [111] which is an honest-majority four party protocol with malicious security. The MPC accelerator includes a pseudorandom number generator and the local shares are communicated through DMA. Approaches like these eliminate latency in environments where parties are colocated in the same data center.

Part III

Real-world Use and Considerations

DOI: 10.1561/9781638283454.ch5

Chapter 5

Applications

With the advent of general purpose foundation models that support modalities like text, images, audio, and video, privacy-preserving AI requires high performance now more than ever. High performance privacy-preserving AI can enable a wide range of such applications where valuable knowledge can be gained from private data without revealing the data to others. We now discuss representative solutions in the fields of healthcare, drug discovery, and consumer applications.

5.1 Introduction

High performance AI is now ubiquitous, with applications permeating into every field. However, in applications where privacy of individuals can potentially get compromised, usage of AI can get hindered. For example, in healthcare, medical records are private and not readily available for use in model training. If data from across healthcare institutions could be leveraged, invaluable insights would undoubtedly be obtained, improving patient care and reducing costs. Examples of privacy-preserving methods for healthcare applications are discussed in Section 5.2.

As another example, multi-party computation (MPC) can also be used in AI-based drug discovery. Drug companies are highly protective of intellectual property but there are situations where all could benefit from collaboration, such as for creating joint models of toxicity prediction. MPC can enable such joint work while still protecting the confidentiality of intellectual property. Section 5.3 discusses applications in drug discovery.

Consumer applications such as IoT (Internet of Things), smart home, personal health tracking, personal finance, and personal digital assistants generate sensitive data that usually end up in the control of corporations that may or may not have protections in place to secure sensitive data. One report [112] says that the number of victims of data breaches reached an all time high in 2023 already by Q3 at around 233 million victims and 2116 compromises. The userbase of a compromised services and the company hosting the data both end up victimized. According to a report by IBM [113], the global average cost for a data breach was USD 4.45 million in 2023. Privacy-preserving technologies are one way to reduce the attack vectors. Section 5.4 discusses consumer applications where high performance privacy-preserving AI technologies are being used.

5.2   Applications in Healthcare

Healthcare data is both highly sensitive and highly treasured as it reveals patterns that can be used for developing better treatments for patients. This section highlights the need for privacy-preserving techniques in healthcare applications and how they are being used in some instances.

5.2.1   Motivation

During the COVID-19 pandemic, it would have been powerful to be able to train predictive models across electronic health records (EHR) early in the pandemic. But healthcare institutions are understandably highly protective of record confidentiality, meaning that traditionally, such work happens within individual hospitals rather than across hospitals.

Questions like the impact of common blood pressure medications should be easy to answer based on the real-world data accumulated in health records. Or consider Ibuprofen. Earlier, the World Health Organization issued a recommendation against the use of Ibuprofen based on reports out of Europe that many younger patients admitted to the hospital with COVID-19 had been taking the popular NSAID (non-steroidal anti-inflammatory drug). But mere days later, they withdrew the recommendation. Issues like this should be possible to probe instantly over large patient record datasets. So too should we have been able to rapidly gain statistically significant insight into the impact of various comorbidities.

With emerging new technologies like MPC/HE, such analysis can be performed without any records leaving each participating institution, bypassing fraught privacy considerations. The authors of this book have demonstrated this with partner institutions [114]. The security model is such that no one can even tell the number of patients meeting a given criteria at the institution. Current practices would require us to wait for one institution to see enough cases or for time consuming manual compilation of results across institutions, a process that frequently takes months. Given the pace of the outbreaks like COVID-19, traditional research timelines are unacceptable. By making patient records immediately available for study—without any sacrifice of institutional or patient privacy whatsoever—the technology enables for findings based on the real-world evidence of patients already seeking care in hospitals.

5.2.2   HE in Healthcare

Homomorphic encryption (HE) is particularly useful for inference. Consider that a private company or academic collaborator has a powerful AI model. As illustrated in Figure 5.1, a hospital can homomorphically encrypt a patient's data and send it to the partner, who will pass it through the model, but will not be able to decrypt the input or the output. The encrypted output is returned to the healthcare institution,

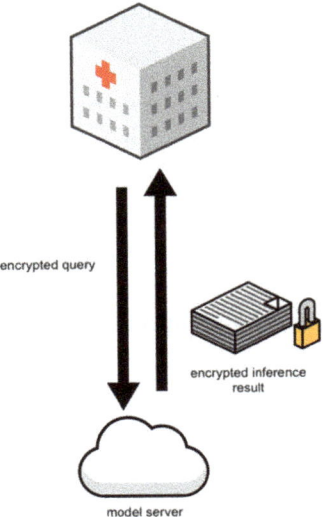

encrypted query

encrypted inference
result

model server

Figure 5.1. A patient's data can be homomorphically encrypted and sent to an outside model provider, who will neither be able to read the query nor result.

where it is decrypted. In this manner, the patient's sensitive information is never exposed to the outside party – and the outside party does not need to share its model with the healthcare institution.

An earlier effort to help advance medical research was made with SecureMed [115], which is an FHE scheme based on an NTRU-variant [116] of GSW [33]. The public-keys are distributed by a key authority system to the server and then to the patients which is then used to encrypt the private data. Results of the computation can then be accessed by research groups through secure channels to the key authority system. They implement solutions for applications such as blood pressure classification, Framingham Coronary Heart Disease Risk Score (FCRS) [117], genotype encoding, and predictive analysis. Their implementation can be accelerated by a multi-GPU setup of four GPUs (NVIDIA GeForce GTX980) and they report a speedup of 104x (or 410x for multi-GPU) over their CPU (Intel Core-i7 5930K) implementation.

CareNets [118] is a FHE library based on GPU-accelerated BFV [31, 32] for abnormality detection of two clinical conditions: Retinopathy of Prematurity (ROP) and Diabetic Retinopathy (DR). By making use of a compact matrix packing strategy implemented as a library, and by designing a resource efficient CNN designed for inference on real-world medical imaging datasets, they perform inference on these tasks which work on images of size 96x96 and 256x256 respectively. On ROP, for security level of 80-bits, they report a speedup of 3.96x on CPU (Intel Xeon Platinum 8170) and 45.9x on GPU (NVIDIA Tesla V100 16GB) compared to the traditional packing strategy used in CryptoNets [119].

5.2.3   MPC in Healthcare

MPC allows for collaboration across multiple parties to compute a function in a privacy-preserving manner. This opens up new avenues for organizations like hospitals, insurers, drug companies, and universities, and for individuals like doctors, patients, and care providers, to team up to build innovative AI models without worrying about privacy of their data. Figure 5.2 illustrates one scenario where MPC can be used. Multiple hospitals can train AI models collaboratively. Once trained, each hospital will have access to the trained model and can perform inference. These trained models benefit from the large number of patients that would otherwise be unavailable.

While developing solutions for applications in areas like healthcare, it is essential that application development is made user-friendly. Sequre [120], an MPC compiler framework, is one such effort in that direction while still being able to use optimized execution to achieve high performance. It follows the principle that compile-time optimizations that utilize domain-specific knowledge can produce optimized

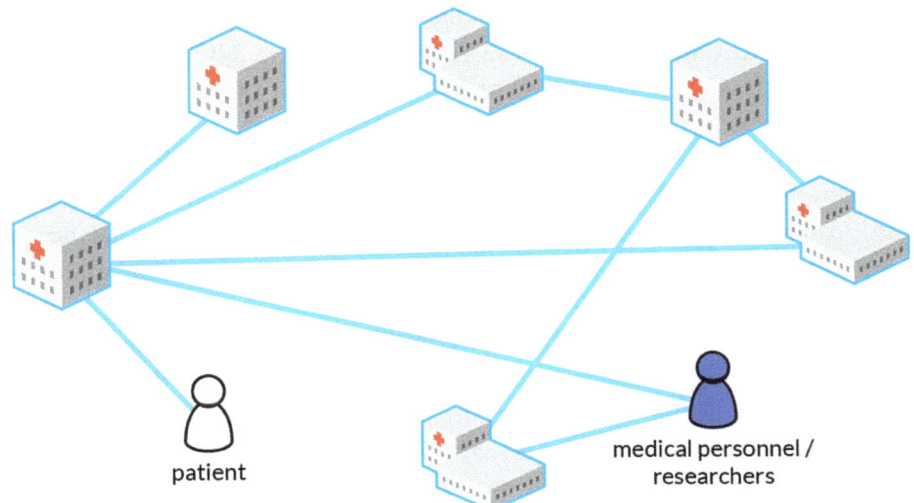

Figure 5.2. MPC can be used to train models across sites, without any sensitive data being exposed from each site to the other parties or anyone else.

executables. By providing the Python decorator @sequre, Sequre automatically converts the enclosed function into an MPC function and also performs MPC related operations to reduce network utilization and runtime performance. It uses additive secret sharing in a four party setting with trusted dealer under honest-but-curious model and it supports common arithmetic, Boolean and linear algebra operations. They demonstrate improvements on usage of this framework on tasks such as genome-wide association studies, drug-target interaction prediction, and metagenomic binning, and report 3–4x increased speed over existing pipelines with 7-fold reduction in codebase size. Neural network functions are also supported and they find that Sequre is 2x faster when compared to PySyft [121] while performing inference on a drug-target interaction prediction model.

When a disease is rare, a single hospital will not have enough data to train predictive models for it. Spini et al. developed a proof-of-concept implementation to assist clinicians to choose optimal treatments for HIV patients based on insights uncovered from previous treatment data [122]. The solution computes an effectiveness measure of an HIV treatment (average time-to-treatment-failure), while preserving privacy. Time-to-treatment-failure is an effectiveness measure in time of days between the start of a therapy and either a therapy switch, discontinuation, or death. They define distance metrics to calculate patient similarity so that the effectiveness of the treatment plan can be estimated. They use SPDZ protocol in a multi-party setting with a) input parties who can issue queries b) clinicians who supply the database records (data owners), and c) computing parties. The output of the computation is presented to the clinician without leaking it to any other parties. Their experimental setup has a i7-7567U CPU with 32GB RAM for each computing party, and a security level of 40-bits (128-bit computational security) in a 128-bit prime field. With this setup, they can compute the solution to a query in 24 minutes for a database of 20000 patient records, which roughly matches the number of patients in the authors' country, the Netherlands, and is considered a realistic database size. Most of the time elapsed in computation is consumed during triple generation taking approximately 22 minutes to generate 40 million multiplication triples.

One of the challenges faced when using MPC protocols in healthcare applications is that not all participants might have the data formatted in the same way. File formats may include comma-separated values, JSON, XML, or proprietary formats. Additionally, column names may vary. In smaller groups of participants, this can be solved by agreeing upon the formats and labels beforehand, but this might take time and effort. Another solution would be to use one of the foundation models like LLMs to predict the meaning of the columns and perform a cleanup of the data beforehand and automatically generate an agreed upon format.

5.3   Applications in Drug Discovery

Figure 5.3 illustrates a scenario for privacy-preserving drug discovery where universities, hospitals, and pharmaceutical companies can collaborate to jointly train

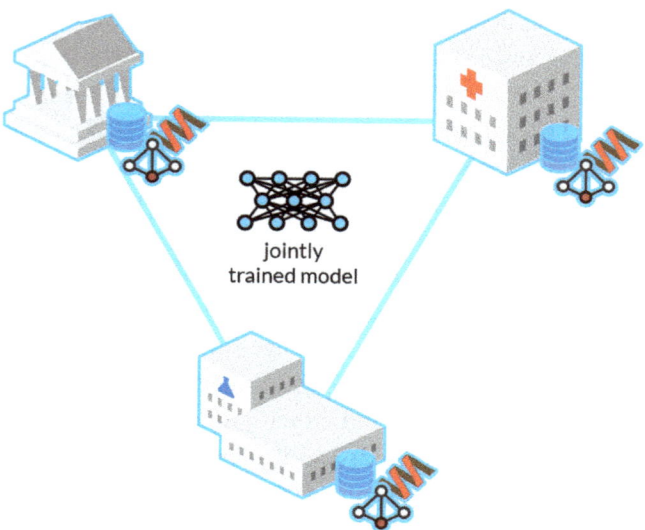

Figure 5.3. In drug discovery too, models may be trained with secure MPC.

neural network-based predictive models via MPC. With a larger pool of data for joint private training between multiple organizations, better AI models can be trained and better conclusions can be drawn without jeopardizing intellectual property.

An earlier work on privacy-preserving drug discovery [123] showcases using SPDZ in a three-party honest-but-curious setting for predicting drug-target interactions (DTI). In their setup the collaborating entities such as pharmaceutical companies or research labs share their large DTI datasets along with chemical and protein structures privately among participating entities via secret sharing and then jointly train a predictive model such as a neural network on it. The final model can then be shared among the participants. With that setting, they demonstrate training a neural network (Secure DTI) on more than 1 million training instances over a WAN (wide area network) in less than 4 days.

Ma et al. develop two neural networks: DTIMPC for privacy-preserving prediction of novel DTIs and QSARMPC for privacy-preserving collaboration on large-scale quantitative structure-activity relationship (QSAR) [124]. This is the first work on collaborative prediction of QSAR with MPC. They use a replicated 2-out-of-4 secret sharing MPC protocol, which is secure for 2 out of 4 semi-honest parties [125]. The authors also note that there are many challenges in doing MPC-based drug discovery across companies and institutions: convincing pharmaceutical companies about collaboration and security, slow execution time, and learning curve.

5.4 Applications in Consumer Applications

Entities in consumer applications are varied, including customers, anonymous computing parties, and third-party server providers, and customers have little insight into who is able to see their most private data.

5.4.1 Wearables

Wearable devices are used for personal health monitoring. They can be used to detect irregular heartbeat, sleep apnea, blood oxygen levels, and falls. All this is possible because of sensors and AI technologies that predict these events based on learned features. This data can also be abused by malicious entities in many ways.

A proof-of-concept study for privacy-preserving atrial fibrillation detection [126] was executed involving the building of a deep learning library for homomorphically encrypted data and then testing it for predicting atrial fibrillation [127]. Atrial fibrillation can be detected by analyzing ECG (electrocardiogram) data that is recorded by wearables and in this work they used the recording from Physionet

2017 challenge [128] as their dataset. The homomorphic encryption scheme they use here is based on MORE (Matrix Operation for Randomization or Encryption) encryption scheme [129]. This is a fully homomorphic scheme but with some drawbacks, such as the inability to perform comparison operations on ciphertext, which impacts implementation of CNN layers such as maxpooling, limited choice in neural network optimizers, and vulnerability to chosen plaintext attack. This vulnerability is not a concern in this scenario, as the plaintext ECG data never leaves the device. They obtain encouraging results from this detection model which achieves high accuracy that is close to the state-of-the-art.

Falls can be detected in various ways [130] using sensors such as accelerometers, inertial measurement unit which is a multi-modal sensor consisting of accelerometer and a gyroscope, camera-based approaches, and ambience-based approaches where sensors are placed in the vicinity. Since falls can vary in many ways depending on environment and the person, fall detection might need substantial processing power and accurate predictions might not be possible on wearable devices thus needing to send the data over to external servers. In that process, the server might learn revealing information about the user such as gait, activities and relative position. To move towards a privacy-preserving approach for fall detection [131], investigates an MPC-based fall detection technique based on various AI techniques to detect falls by using data from an IMU sensor. Using publicly available datasets provided by SmartFall [132], they achieve state-of-the-art error rates with their SVM classifier with their derivative-based features. They find that the total prediction time is less than the on-device acquisition time, which makes real-time fall detection via MPC a possibility. They adopt arithmetic secret sharing based MPC in honest-but-curious setting that supports an arbitrary number of parties (3 for experiments) using MPyc [133].

5.4.2 IoT

IoT devices are ubiquitous in our lives but they can be invasive in terms of privacy as the sensors in these devices collect private data. Manufacturers and service providers use this data for constantly improving the performance of AI applications enabled through and for IoT but in that process, the data can be abused in many ways. An example of that is the recent controversy resulting from Ring's handling of customer's private home security videos [134]. Training and inference with privacy-preserving technologies such as HE and MPC is one of the ways to protect consumers against issues like this.

A GPU accelerated FHE-based runtime library was proposed that can perform inference of neural network models with high accuracy in real-time for IoT applications. Li et al. developed a confused-modulo projection [135] based FHE and

RT-HCNN (real-time homomorphic CNN) network that can perform a GPU-accelerated (NVIDIA RTX 3090) MNIST inference with 99.13% accuracy in 79.5ms, with security level of 192-bits [136].

A challenge with the use of HE in IoT applications is that the edge devices on the client-side are not as capable as servers, and thus might not offer the kind of performance needed for fast encryption and decryption of ciphertext. Works such as RISE [137] have attempted to close that gap. RISE is an ASIC solution that is 6191.19x more energy efficient for CKKS encryption, and 2481.44x more energy efficient for CKKS decryption, than a RISC-V processor. It makes applications like homomorphically encrypted QVGA-size video streaming possible. Aloha-HE [138] offers an FPGA solution that can perform these edge encryption operations by a factor of up to 59x compared to RISE.

DOI: 10.1561/9781638283454.ch6

Chapter 6

Blockchain and Zero Knowledge Proofs

Blockchain and zero-knowledge (ZK) proof techniques have advanced greatly in recent years, largely spurred by cryptocurrency development. They enable decentralized coordination of, and proofs of computational integrity in, the execution of privacy-preserving protocols.

6.1 Introduction

Bookkeeping is an important part of digital transactions. Protocols based on blockchains were first proposed by David Chaum [139]. Blockchains provide a distributed ledger on which consensus may be obtained without appeal to a trusted authority. Bitcoin [140] was pioneering and triggered an explosion in the development of consensus techniques and real-world blockchains.

Meanwhile, ZK proofs allow a party to prove to another party that a statement is true, without disclosing any information beyond the truth of a statement [141, 142]. ZK proofs of knowledge furthermore allow the prover to demonstrate knowledge of the witness to a particular statement's truth. For example, one can prove that one knows the secret preimage of a given hash, without disclosing that preimage. ZK proof techniques are developing by leaps and bounds, and non-interactive succinct ZK proofs are already commonly used in the context of cryptocurrencies such as Zcash [143]. The proofs are not only succinct, but also highly efficient to verify. Furthermore, consider that one can phrase the execution of a statement to be proven in a ZK proof. With this, ZK can be used to ensure that MPC-based computations are performed correctly by each party.

By combining blockchain and ZK proofs, one can extend privacy-preserving computation to greater numbers of parties, while still being able to ensure computational integrity. They remove the need for a central trusted authority, providing for greater privacy and eliminating the risk of the trusted node being compromised.

Section 6.2 goes into the origin of blockchain technologies and highlights its usage in privacy-preserving techniques. Other cryptographic techniques like hashing, Merkle trees and smart contracts are also introduced. The next Section 6.3 discusses various ZK proof techniques. Finally, Section 6.4 showcases how high performance privacy-preserving AI techniques can be scaled by the use of blockchain and zero-knowledge protocols.

6.2   Blockchain

Simple blockchains consist of a chain of blocks on which consensus has been formed. Each block contains the hash of the previous block, meaning that any attempt to alter the prior history would invalidate all blocks subsequent to the invalidation. A blockchain may also be structured as a decentralized acyclic graph rather than a single linear chain.

In-depth discussion of consensus methods are beyond the scope of this chapter, and we simply note that notable varieties include Byzantine fault tolerant (BFT) methods, typically requiring 2/3 of the set of validators to be honest, and Nakamoto "longest chain" consensus, where the blockchain with the most valid blocks wins. Chains may be secured by proof of work, proof of stake, proof of time, and/or proof of space. With proof of work, for example, adding a block requires the achievement of a computational result (such as a hash meeting given criteria) requiring expenditure of energy, and thus rewriting history would requiring a similar expenditure (during which time the "true" chain is continuing to grow).

6.2.1   Merkle Proofs

Merkle trees facilitate proofs of membership. They can easily be used in zero-knowledge proofs, as discussed in Section 6.3.

Figure 6.1 illustrates a small Merkle tree where the leaves of the tree represent blocks of data D. Data such as files can be large and thus are split into blocks

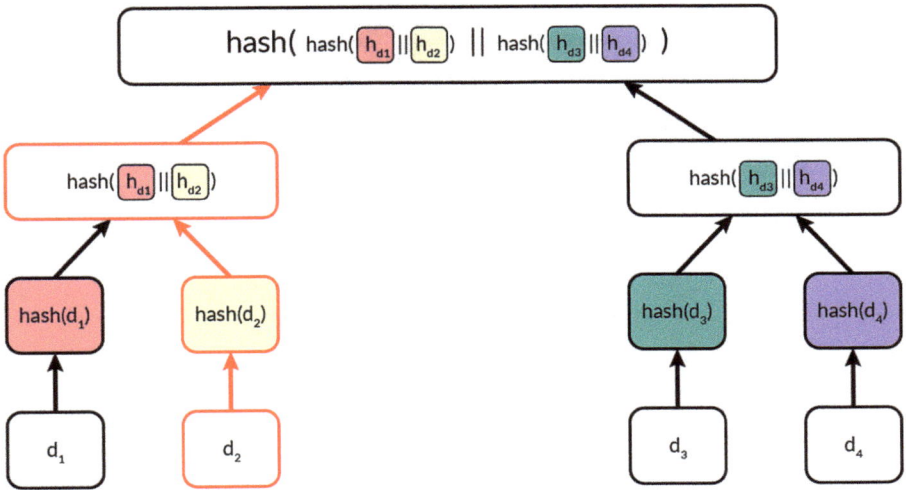

Figure 6.1. Merkle tree and Merkle proof.

d_1, d_2, d_3, d_4. Each non-leaf node in the tree is labeled with the hash of its two children. This means that the root of the tree has a value that is dependent upon, and captures, all leafs. To prove membership of a leaf, one can provide the path of hash pairs from that leaf and its immediate sibling, up to the root. A so-called Merkle proof is therefore logarithmic in the size of the set.

Consider a large file chunked into thousands of pieces. Given the root of the Merkle tree that is constructed from those chunks, one can efficiently show that a given chunk is indeed part of the file.

6.2.2 Smart Contracts

Smart contracts are programs that can reside on a blockchain that automate the process of mediation, payments, services, and actions upon satisfying certain conditions that is dictated by the program. They were proposed by Nick Szabo [144].

Privacy-preserving AI can take advantage of smart contracts to establish digital contracts among participating nodes. For example, contracts can demand satisfaction of certain criteria, such as model accuracy or response time in the protocol, for payment to be released.

Figure 6.2 illustrates an example of how smart contracts can enable transactions on the blockchain. Here is how it plays out:

1. A service provider denoted by the blue meeple creates a smart contract and deploys it to the blockchain. The smart contract has some rules and automation setup for price for the service and then fulfillment of the service.

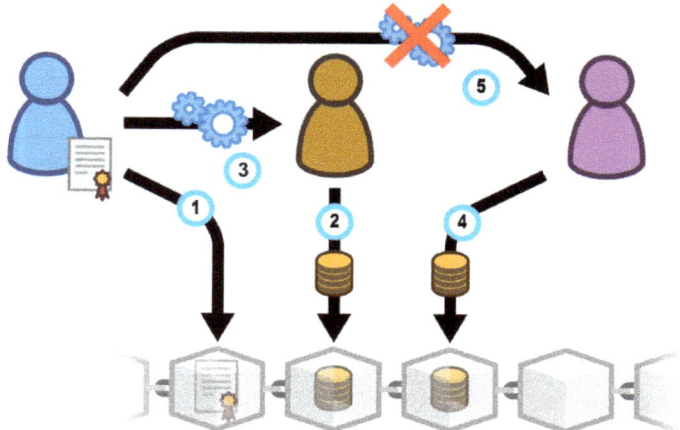

Figure 6.2. Illustration of smart contracts.

2. Another participant yellow, who wants the service, pays a certain amount via a transaction on the blockchain.
3. The smart contract executes successfully, with the service provided and payment released to the provider.
4. The purple client wants the service as well and makes a transaction on the blockchain. This time, there is an unmet condition in the smart contract execution.
5. The contract is not satisfied, so the payment is subsequently returned back to purple and no service is provided.

6.2.3 Hash Functions

A hash function in cryptography is a function with three properties [145]:

1. Preimage-resistance: It is computationally infeasible to find the preimage m of a hash $h = H(m)$.
2. Second-preimage resistance: It is computationally infeasible to find a message $m' \neq m$ such that $H(m) = H(m')$.
3. Collision resistance: It is computationally infeasible to find messages m_1 and m_2 such that $H(m_1) = H(m_2)$.

Collision resistance implies second-preimage resistance but does not guarantee preimage resistance [146].

Special hash functions are being designed and actively used in ZK proofs that improve proving time as the common hashing algorithms like SHA-2, SHA-3 are known to be slow for ZK proving [147].

6.3   Proofs of Knowledge

A proof of knowledge must satisfy two properties.

- Completeness: An honest verifier should be convinced by a proof of a true statement provided by an honest prover. Many commonly-used proof systems are perfectly complete.
- Soundness: A dishonest prover cannot convince an honest verifier of an untrue statement. Succinct so-called *arguments* of knowledge are often computationally sound: sound given a set of hardness assumptions.

    If the proof is a zero-knowledge proof, it must satisfy the additional property of zero knowledge: the verifier learns nothing except the fact that the statement is true.

The literature contains established methods for proving that a particular zero knowledge proof system has the knowledge soundness and zero knowledge properties, but discussing these is beyond the scope of this work. The interested reader is referred to Thaler et al. [148] for more information.

6.3.1   Assumptions and Models Used in ZK

Most practical instantiations of ZK proofs rely on certain cryptographic hardness assumptions for their security, including soundness and zero-knowledge. Common assumptions include the standard assumptions regarding cryptographic hash functions, the hardness of the discrete logarithm, and various hardness results around pairings of elliptic curves.

While a full discussion of the various assumptions commonly invoked is beyond the scope of this text, we note here that certain assumptions, such as the security of cryptographic hash functions, can be instantiated such that they are plausibly secure in the face of large quantum computers, while others, such as the discrete logarithm, would fall in the face of such a threat.

6.3.2   Non-interactive ZK Proofs

A ZK proof can be interactive or non-interactive. Interactive proofs need back and forth communication between the prover and verifier, which is not so in the case of non-interactive proofs. In interactive ZK proofs, a verifier can offer multiple challenges to the prover to convince themselves that the prover in fact is in possession of the witness. Once the verifier reaches a desired level of certainty, the prover is believed to be in possession of witness. It should be noted that analyzing the soundness of such multi-round proofs can be a very complex exercise. Finally, interactive proofs are limited in the contexts in which they can be used, and non-interactive proofs are often better suited to decentralized situations.

6.3.3   Setup

Some proof systems, such as Groth16 [149], require a possibly circuit-specific setup to generate data for future invocations of the prover and verifier. Furthermore, in some systems, the setup is non-transparent, that is, in addition to generating the public reference data, it also generates data that must be deleted. This so-called "toxic waste" can be used to compromise the security of future proofs, and so it is essential that it be deleted. In a decentralized setting, such toxic waste can be mitigated by using secure multiparty computation for the setup, or by using a proof system that does not require such a trusted setup, such as ZK-STARKs [150].

6.3.4   Recursive Proofs

In the case where a verifier has considerably lower complexity than the prover, a natural question arises: is it possible to prove one step at a time (or many in parallel), and then prove the execution of the verifier in another proof to "aggregate" the initial proofs? The answer is yes, and this practice—recursion—significantly decreases memory complexity and enhances parallelism for provers, opening the door to proofs of much larger statements. Some systems, such as Nova [151], are even specifically designed with recursion in mind, having very simple verifiers when expressed in their native constraint systems. While it is beyond the scope of this book to discuss in detail, we note that the addition of recursion to ZK systems can considerably complicate proofs of knowledge soundness.

6.3.5   Pairing-based SNARKs

Pairing-based ZK-SNARKs, often simply referred to as "SNARKs" in the literature, are among the first general zero knowledge proof systems to become popular. They require a trusted setup 6.3.3, but produce extremely small proofs, less than 300 bytes. They accept statements in the form of Rank-1 Constraint Systems [148], and have a fairly complex set of cryptographic assumptions.

Zcash [143] is a pioneering user of SNARKs, and other cryptocurrency ecosystems, like Ethereum [152] and Loopring [153], also make use of them.

6.3.6   STARK (Zero-Knowledge Scalable Transparent Argument of Knowledge)

STARKs [150] are a family of ZK proofs that do not need a trusted setup and are plausibly quantum safe, as the only cryptographic assumption is the existence of cryptographically secure hash functions. They also enjoy small proof size (on the order of 100kB), verification complexity that is polylogarithmic in the size of the witness, and a prover whose complexity is quasilinear in the size of the witness. Statements to be proven in a ZK-STARK take the form of an AIR, which represents a succinct, low-degree transition function that is repeatedly applied. However, it should be noted that for larger witnesses, the quasilinear prover complexity leads to very high memory demands on the prover. As a result, many modern efforts in ZK-STARKs revolve around recursion 6.3.4.

6.3.7   Nova

Another relatively new and popular proof sytem is Nova [151], supporting constraints in R1CS. The core concept in Nova is first to express its own verifier very succinctly as an R1CS. Then, the statement of interest is proven, then the two different instances are "folded" into a single instance. This process can be repeated many times, allowing prover memory demand to remain very low, as well as allowing prover complexity to vary with the length of the proof. Because of its extreme efficiency with recursion, statements used with Nova are often so-called step circuits, that is, intended to be applied repeatedly, each taking the output of the previous as its input. In its current instantiation, Nova relies on the security of the discrete log problem.

In recent years, ZK proofs have become practical for a large class of statements, especially with the introduction of recursion. In principle, they can be used directly to prove to a counterparty that a particular task has been performed correctly. However, there are several difficulties. First, the problem statement must be described in relatively unnatural languages such as Rank-1 Constraint Systems (R1CS) [148] or Algebraic Intermediate Representation (AIR) [148], both of which are far removed from even low-level programming. Second, even though the performance of zero-knowledge proofs has drastically improved, they are still difficult to use on tasks as large as deep neural networks, which may contain hundreds of millions of multiplications (a key measure of complexity) or more. The following subsection offers some solutions for more practical ZK proving.

6.3.8   Practical ZKP

In addition to prover performance, a major obstacle to practical ZK proofs is the need to express the statement of interest in an unusual language, such as R1CS or AIR. However, there are several recent developments that have eased this burden. One is tooling, akin to high-level hardware description languages, that can compile programmer-friendly languages down to constraint systems. These include

Noir [154], Zokrates [155], and Circom [156], among others. However, though they ease the burden of developing constraint systems, several difficulties remain. For instance, conditionals must always evaluate both branches, and loops without compile-time bounds are forbidden.

To alleviate this challenge, some groups, including the authors, are developing or have developed so-called Zero Knowledge Virtual Machines (ZKVMs). These ZKVMs provide a constraint system for a virtual version of a CPU, which can be targeted by standard programming languages such as C or Rust or unique languages that nonetheless retain capabilities such as branching and unbounded looping.

Cairo [157] is a virtual machine implemented as a zero-knowledge proof platform. This allows it to target arbitrary programs to a virtual machine, without worrying about constructing new algebraic representations for each new problem. It offers a Rust-like language for programming and supports generation of STARK proofs of execution.

RISC Zero [158] is another ZKVM that opens up the RISC-V microarchitecture for ZK proofs. It allows developers to write Rust programs and potentially any language that compiles to RISC-V to write ZK proofs. Additionally, it also allows for GPU and Apple Metal acceleration.

To address performance, ZK proofs can be accelerated by GPUs, FPGAs, or ASICs. Particular steps during proving and verification such as polynomial evaluation and interpolation of STARKs are usually targeted for acceleration as they are performed with FFT/NTT which can be accelerated easily. Multiscalar multiplication is another common target for GPU acceleration in proof systems for which it is relevant. GPU accelerated libraries such as Winterfell [159] for STARKs written in Rust, ICICLE [160] which is a general purpose library for ZK proofs written in C++ with Rust and Go bindings, *bellperson* [161] which is a GPU-accelerated SNARK library based on *bellman* [162], and *ezkl* [163] which is a Rust-based SNARK library for inferencing deep learning models and computational graphs. There are also special purpose hardware (ASICs that have been referred to as "ZPUs" [164]), such as PipeZK [165], which is a 28nm chip that can achieve 10x speedup on SNARKs on standard benchmarks and 5x speedup on Zcash [143].

6.4   Enhancing Privacy at Scale with Blockchain and ZK

Collaborating across multiple organizations for privacy-preserving AI tasks can be a daunting task as it can present a wide range of challenges, such as unfaithful or malicious parties trying to either gain information without giving anything back, or trying to thwart the whole process by sharing false or malicious data to throw off the statistics, or simply not performing expensive parts of the computation honestly.

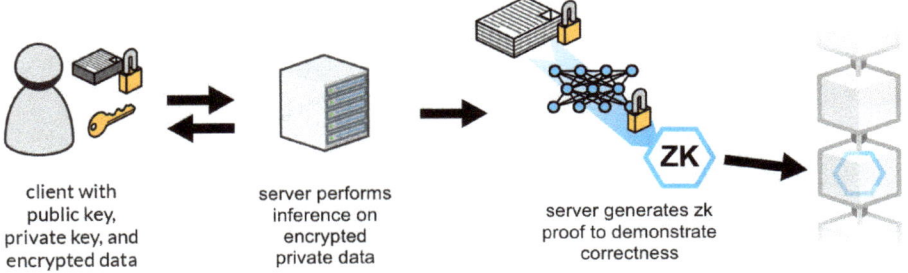

client with
public key,
private key, and
encrypted data

server performs
inference on
encrypted
private data

server generates zk
proof to demonstrate
correctness

Figure 6.3. A verifiable and auditable homomorphic encryption system.

Using blockchain technologies and cryptographic proof systems described above provides a solution to these problems by allowing the detection of malicious activity.

6.4.1   Verifiable and Auditable Homomorphic Encryption

A verifiable and auditable privacy-preserving system that can handle AI applications such as neural network inference is shown in Figure 6.3. The client creates homomorphic encryption keys and encrypts their private data with the keys. The server is a service provider or a node on the cloud or the internet that offers inference of neural networks or any other such computation. The server stores execution steps/trace of its computation and subsequently generates a ZK proof out of it. A commitment to the ZK proof can be then published to allow the client or anyone with access to the blockchain to verify that the server performed the computation correctly. Such a system was developed and demonstrated by the authors for performing secure inference of neural networks on private data.

This system can also account for payment systems. If server expects a fee from the client for the computation, the server can set up a smart contract on the blockchain that dictates that on a successful, faithful and correct training of the neural network, server gets the payment from the client.

6.4.2   Verifiable and Auditable MPC

Figure 6.4 illustrates a verifiable and auditable MPC framework where nodes use their private data to perform MPC and, while doing so, store execution traces so that ZK proofs can be generated. Each party publishes commitments to the blockchain that reflect the proofs. Anyone who has access to the blockchain commitments can check whether each party performed their part of the training correctly. We are leveraging such a framework for training of neural networks across multiple institutions.

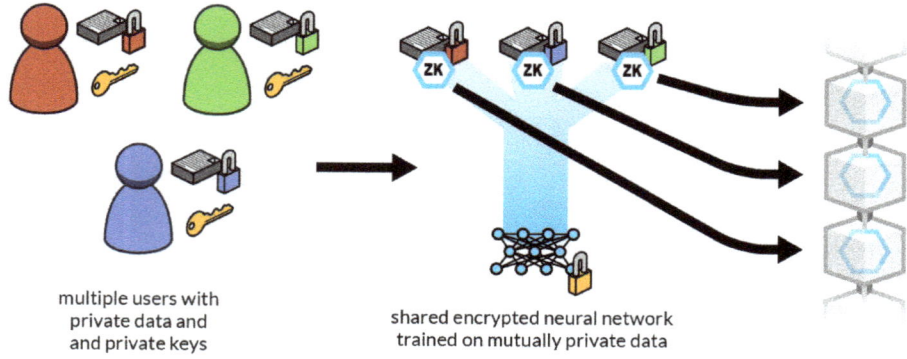

multiple users with
private data and
and private keys

shared encrypted neural network
trained on mutually private data

Figure 6.4. A verifiable and auditable MPC.

Payment systems can also be incorporated where each party is compensated for its share of their training.

Training of neural networks with MPC is thus possible in a verifiable manner that maintains the privacy of all parties' data and allows them to be paid for proper participation.

There have been recent works incorporating blockchain technologies and ZK proofs for computational integrity and auditing. Healthlock [166] enabled blockchain-based homomorphic encryption for training of deep neural networks on IoT data. It enforces fine-grained access control through blockchain and smart contracts ensuring that only authorized users can access sensitive encrypted data. Zhang et al. trained encrypted neural networks on the IRIS dataset [167], such that anyone in possession of the proof of training generated from the ZKVM can verify if the learning nodes performed the training correctly [168].

DOI: 10.1561/9781638283454.ch7

Chapter 7

Conclusion

Techniques for accelerating privacy-preserving AI are opening a new era unhindered by tension between utilizing data and maintaining privacy.

As discussed, applications are already arising in fields such as healthcare, drug discovery, wearable technologies, home security, and more. Challenges in organizing a large-scale collaboration can be addressed with blockchain and ZK proof technologies. The space is rapidly progressing.

This book showcased the current state of high performance privacy-preserving techniques when applied to AI applications and it also provided a look into the future where these techniques can be applied in large scale distributed and decentralized environments. We hope the reader helps advance this exciting future.

References

[1] R. L. Rivest, L. Adleman, M. L. Dertouzos, *et al.*, "On data banks and privacy homomorphisms," *Foundations of secure computation*, vol. 4, no. 11, pp. 169–180, 1978.

[2] R. L. Rivest, A. Shamir, and L. Adleman, "A method for obtaining digital signatures and public-key cryptosystems," *Commun. ACM*, vol. 21, p. 120–126, feb 1978.

[3] C. Gentry, "Fully homomorphic encryption using ideal lattices," in *Proceedings of the Forty-First Annual ACM Symposium on Theory of Computing*, STOC '09, (New York, NY, USA), p. 169–178, Association for Computing Machinery, 2009.

[4] O. Regev, "On lattices, learning with errors, random linear codes, and cryptography," *J. ACM*, vol. 56, sep 2009.

[5] P. Paillier, "Public-key cryptosystems based on composite degree residuosity classes," in *Advances in Cryptology – EUROCRYPT '99* (J. Stern, ed.), (Berlin, Heidelberg), pp. 223–238, Springer Berlin Heidelberg, 1999.

[6] J. Wang, C. Jin, S. Meftah, and K. M. M. Aung, "Popcorn: Paillier meets compression for efficient oblivious neural network inference," 2021.

[7] J. Deng, W. Dong, R. Socher, L.-J. Li, K. Li, and L. Fei-Fei, "Imagenet: A large-scale hierarchical image database," in *2009 IEEE Conference on Computer Vision and Pattern Recognition*, pp. 248–255, 2009.

[8] R. W. Hamming, "Error detecting and error correcting codes," *The Bell System Technical Journal*, vol. 29, no. 2, pp. 147–160, 1950.

[9] M. Rabin, "How to exchange secrets with oblivious transfer," *IACR Cryptology ePrint Archive*, vol. 2005, p. 187, 01 2005.

[10] Y. Ma, L. Wu, X. Gu, J. He, and Z. Yang, "A secure face-verification scheme based on homomorphic encryption and deep neural networks," *IEEE Access*, vol. 5, pp. 16532–16538, 2017.

[11] Y. LeCun and C. Cortes, "MNIST handwritten digit database," 2010.

[12] A. Krizhevsky, V. Nair, and G. Hinton, "Cifar-10 (canadian institute for advanced research),"

[13] Q. Lou and L. Jiang, "She: A fast and accurate deep neural network for encrypted data," in *Advances in Neural Information Processing Systems* (H. Wallach, H. Larochelle, A. Beygelzimer, F. d'Alché-Buc, E. Fox, and R. Garnett, eds.), vol. 32, Curran Associates, Inc., 2019.

[14] K. He, X. Zhang, S. Ren, and J. Sun, "Deep residual learning for image recognition," 2015.

[15] A. Krizhevsky, I. Sutskever, and G. E. Hinton, "Imagenet classification with deep convolutional neural networks," in *Proceedings of the 25th International Conference on Neural Information Processing Systems – Volume 1*, NIPS'12, (Red Hook, NY, USA), p. 1097–1105, Curran Associates Inc., 2012.

[16] X. Zhang, X. Zhou, M. Lin, and J. Sun, "Shufflenet: An extremely efficient convolutional neural network for mobile devices," in *2018 IEEE/CVF Conference on Computer Vision and Pattern Recognition*, pp. 6848–6856, 2018.

[17] S. Hochreiter and J. Schmidhuber, "Long short-term memory," *Neural Comput.*, vol. 9, p. 1735–1780, nov 1997.

[18] M. P. Marcus, B. Santorini, and M. A. Marcinkiewicz, "Building a large annotated corpus of English: The Penn Treebank," *Computational Linguistics*, vol. 19, no. 2, pp. 313–330, 1993.

[19] J. H. Cheon, A. Kim, M. Kim, and Y. Song, "Homomorphic encryption for arithmetic of approximate numbers," in *Advances in Cryptology – ASIACRYPT 2017* (T. Takagi and T. Peyrin, eds.), (Cham), pp. 409–437, Springer International Publishing, 2017.

[20] J. H. Cheon, K. Han, A. Kim, M. Kim, and Y. Song, "Bootstrapping for approximate homomorphic encryption," in *Advances in Cryptology – EUROCRYPT 2018* (J. B. Nielsen and V. Rijmen, eds.), (Cham), pp. 360–384, Springer International Publishing, 2018.

[21] W. Jung, E. Lee, S. Kim, J. Kim, N. Kim, K. Lee, C. Min, J. H. Cheon, and J. H. Ahn, "Accelerating fully homomorphic encryption through architecture-centric analysis and optimization," *IEEE Access*, vol. 9, pp. 98772–98789, 2021.

[22] J.-W. Lee, E. Lee, Y. Lee, Y.-S. Kim, and J.-S. No, "High-precision bootstrapping of rns-ckks homomorphic encryption using optimal minimax polynomial approximation and inverse sine function," in *Advances in Cryptology – EUROCRYPT 2021* (A. Canteaut and F.-X. Standaert, eds.), (Cham), pp. 618–647, Springer International Publishing, 2021.

[23] A. A. Badawi, L. Hoang, C. F. Mun, K. Laine, and K. M. M. Aung, "Privft: Private and fast text classification with homomorphic encryption," *IEEE Access*, vol. 8, pp. 226544–226556, 2020.

[24] J.-W. Lee, H. Kang, Y. Lee, W. Choi, J. Eom, M. Deryabin, E. Lee, J. Lee, D. Yoo, Y.-S. Kim, and J.-S. No, "Privacy-preserving machine learning with fully homomorphic encryption for deep neural network," *IEEE Access*, vol. 10, pp. 30039–30054, 2022.

[25] J. Devlin, M.-W. Chang, K. Lee, and K. Toutanova, "BERT: Pre-training of deep bidirectional transformers for language understanding," in *Proceedings of the 2019 Conference of the North American Chapter of the Association for Computational Linguistics: Human Language Technologies, Volume 1 (Long and Short Papers)* (J. Burstein, C. Doran, and T. Solorio, eds.), (Minneapolis, Minnesota), pp. 4171–4186, Association for Computational Linguistics, June 2019.

[26] I. Chillotti, N. Gama, M. Georgieva, and M. Izabachène, "Tfhe: Fast fully homomorphic encryption over the torus," Cryptology ePrint Archive, Paper 2018/421, 2018. https://eprint.iacr.org/2018/421.

[27] L. Ducas and D. Micciancio, "Fhew: Bootstrapping homomorphic encryption in less than a second," in *Advances in Cryptology – EUROCRYPT 2015* (E. Oswald and M. Fischlin, eds.), (Berlin, Heidelberg), pp. 617–640, Springer Berlin Heidelberg, 2015.

[28] I. Chillotti, D. Ligier, J.-B. Orfila, and S. Tap, "Improved programmable bootstrapping with larger precision and efficient arithmetic circuits for TFHE," in *Advances in Cryptology – ASIACRYPT 2021* (M. Tibouchi and H. Wang, eds.), (Cham), pp. 670–699, Springer International Publishing, 2021.

[29] "TFHE Deep Dive – Part I – Ciphertext types – zama.ai." https://www.zama.ai/post/tfhe-deep-dive-part-1. [Accessed 29-12-2023].

[30] Z. Brakerski, C. Gentry, and V. Vaikuntanathan, "(leveled) fully homomorphic encryption without bootstrapping," in *Proceedings of the 3rd Innovations in Theoretical Computer Science Conference*, ITCS '12, (New York, NY, USA), p. 309–325, Association for Computing Machinery, 2012.

[31] Z. Brakerski, "Fully homomorphic encryption without modulus switching from classical gapsvp," in *Advances in Cryptology – CRYPTO 2012* (R. Safavi-Naini and R. Canetti, eds.), (Berlin, Heidelberg), pp. 868–886, Springer Berlin Heidelberg, 2012.

[32] J. Fan and F. Vercauteren, "Somewhat practical fully homomorphic encryption," *IACR Cryptol. ePrint Arch.*, p. 144, 2012.

[33] C. Gentry, A. Sahai, and B. Waters, "Homomorphic encryption from learning with errors: Conceptually-simpler, asymptotically-faster, attribute-based," in *Advances in Cryptology – CRYPTO 2013* (R. Canetti and J. A. Garay, eds.), (Berlin, Heidelberg), pp. 75–92, Springer Berlin Heidelberg, 2013.

[34] M. Albrecht, R. Player, and S. Scott, "On the concrete hardness of learning with errors," *Journal of Mathematical Cryptology*, vol. 9, 10 2015.

[35] A. Stoian, J. Frery, R. Bredehoft, L. Montero, C. Kherfallah, and B. Chevallier-Mames, "Deep neural networks for encrypted inference with tfhe," in *Cyber Security, Cryptology, and Machine Learning* (S. Dolev, E. Gudes, and P. Paillier, eds.), (Cham), pp. 493–500, Springer Nature Switzerland, 2023.

[36] A. Meyre, B. Chevallier-Mames, J. Frery, A. Stoian, R. Bredehoft, L. Montero, and C. Kherfallah, "Concrete ML: a privacy-preserving machine learning library using fully homomorphic encryption for data scientists," 2022. https://github.com/zama-ai/concrete-ml.

[37] M. Albrecht, M. Chase, H. Chen, J. Ding, S. Goldwasser, S. Gorbunov, S. Halevi, J. Hoffstein, K. Laine, K. Lauter, S. Lokam, D. Micciancio, D. Moody, T. Morrison, A. Sahai, and V. Vaikuntanathan, "Homomorphic encryption security standard," tech. rep., HomomorphicEncryption.org, Toronto, Canada, November 2018.

[38] "IT Security techniques – Encryption algorithms – Part 6: Homomorphic encryption," standard, International Organization for Standardization, Geneva, CH, May 2019.

[39] J. Devlin, M.-W. Chang, K. Lee, and K. Toutanova, "BERT: Pre-training of deep bidirectional transformers for language understanding," in *Proceedings of the 2019 Conference of the North American Chapter of the Association for Computational Linguistics: Human Language Technologies, Volume 1 (Long and Short Papers)* (J. Burstein, C. Doran, and T. Solorio, eds.), (Minneapolis, Minnesota), pp. 4171–4186, Association for Computational Linguistics, June 2019.

[40] A. Vaswani, N. M. Shazeer, N. Parmar, J. Uszkoreit, L. Jones, A. N. Gomez, L. Kaiser, and I. Polosukhin, "Attention is all you need," in *Neural Information Processing Systems*, 2017.

[41] G. Gerganov, "GitHub – ggerganov/llama.cpp: Port of Facebook's LLaMA model in C/C++ – github.com." https://github.com/ggerganov/llama.cpp. [Accessed 21-01-2024].

[42] turboderp, "GitHub – turboderp/exllama: A more memory-efficient rewrite of the HF transformers implementation of Llama for use with quantized

weights. – github.com." https://github.com/turboderp/exllama. [Accessed 21-01-2024].

[43] A. C.-C. Yao, "How to generate and exchange secrets," in *27th Annual Symposium on Foundations of Computer Science (sfcs 1986)*, pp. 162–167, 1986.

[44] A. Shamir, "How to share a secret.," *Communications of the ACM*, vol. 22, no. 11, pp. 612–613, 1979.

[45] D. Beaver, "Efficient multiparty protocols using circuit randomization," in *Advances in Cryptology – CRYPTO '91, 11th Annual International Cryptology Conference, Santa Barbara, California, USA, August 11–15, 1991, Proceedings*, vol. 576 of *Lecture Notes in Computer Science*, pp. 420–432, Springer, 1991.

[46] I. Damgård, V. Pastro, N. P. Smart, and S. Zakarias, "Multiparty computation from somewhat homomorphic encryption," in *Advances in Cryptology – Crypto 2012*, vol. 7417 of *Lecture Notes in Computer Science*, pp. 643–662, Springer, 2012.

[47] I. Damgård, M. Keller, E. Larraia, V. Pastro, P. Scholl, and N. P. Smart, "Practical covertly secure mpc for dishonest majority – or: Breaking the spdz limits," in *Computer Security – ESORICS 2013* (J. Crampton, S. Jajodia, and K. Mayes, eds.), (Berlin, Heidelberg), pp. 1–18, Springer Berlin Heidelberg, 2013.

[48] "SPDZ blog series," http://bristolcrypto.blogspot.com/2016/10/what-is-spdz-part-1-mpc-circuit.html.

[49] B. Knott, S. Venkataraman, A. Hannun, S. Sengupta, M. Ibrahim, and L. van der Maaten, "Crypten: Secure multi-party computation meets machine learning," in *arXiv 2109.00984*, 2021.

[50] A. Paszke, S. Gross, F. Massa, A. Lerer, J. Bradbury, G. Chanan, T. Killeen, Z. Lin, N. Gimelshein, L. Antiga, A. Desmaison, A. Köpf, E. Yang, Z. DeVito, M. Raison, A. Tejani, S. Chilamkurthy, B. Steiner, L. Fang, J. Bai, and S. Chintala, "Pytorch: An imperative style, high-performance deep learning library," 2019.

[51] S. Adams, D. Melanson, and M. De Cock, "Private text classification with convolutional neural networks," in *Proceedings of the Third Workshop on Privacy in Natural Language Processing*, pp. 53–58, 2021.

[52] M. Keller, E. Orsini, and P. Scholl, "Mascot: Faster malicious arithmetic secure computation with oblivious transfer," in *Proceedings of the 2016 ACM SIGSAC Conference on Computer and Communications Security*, CCS '16, (New York, NY, USA), p. 830–842, Association for Computing Machinery, 2016.

[53] Intel, "Intel® architecture instruction set extensions programming reference," https://www.intel.com/content/dam/develop/external/us/en/d ocuments/319433-024-697869.pdf, 2016.

[54] M. Keller, "MP-SPDZ: A versatile framework for multi-party computation," in *Proceedings of the 2020 ACM SIGSAC Conference on Computer and Communications Security*, 2020.

[55] data61, "A versatile framework for multi-party computation," https://gith ub.com/data61/MP-SPDZ. GitHub.

[56] Z. Huang, W. jie Lu, C. Hong, and J. Ding, "Cheetah: Lean and fast secure Two-Party deep neural network inference," in *31st USENIX Security Symposium (USENIX Security 22)*, (Boston, MA), pp. 809–826, USENIX Association, Aug. 2022.

[57] P. Rindal, "The ABY3 Framework for Machine Learning and Database Operations," https://github.com/ladnir/aby3.

[58] A. Dalskov, D. Escudero, and M. Keller, "Fantastic four:{Honest-Majority}{Four-Party} secure computation with malicious security," in *30th USENIX Security Symposium (USENIX Security 21)*, pp. 2183–2200, 2021.

[59] S. Tan, B. Knott, Y. Tian, and D. J. Wu, "CryptGPU: Fast privacy-preserving machine learning on the gpu," in *IEEE S&P*, 2021.

[60] Y. Dong, W. jie Lu, Y. Zheng, H. Wu, D. Zhao, J. Tan, Z. Huang, C. Hong, T. Wei, and W. Chen, "Puma: Secure inference of llama-7b in five minutes," 2023.

[61] H. Touvron, T. Lavril, G. Izacard, X. Martinet, M.-A. Lachaux, T. Lacroix, B. Rozière, N. Goyal, E. Hambro, F. Azhar, A. Rodriguez, A. Joulin, E. Grave, and G. Lample, "Llama: Open and efficient foundation language models," 2023.

[62] D. Li, R. Shao, H. Wang, H. Guo, E. P. Xing, and H. Zhang, "Mpcformer: fast, performant and private transformer inference with mpc," *arXiv preprint arXiv:2211.01452*, 2022.

[63] Intel, "Intel® architecture instruction set extensions programming reference," https://www.intel.com/content/dam/develop/external/us/en/d ocuments/319433-024-697869.pdf, 2016.

[64] G. E. Moore, "Cramming more components onto integrated circuits, reprinted from electronics, volume 38, number 8, april 19, 1965, pp.114 ff.," *IEEE Solid-State Circuits Society Newsletter*, vol. 11, no. 3, pp. 33–35, 2006.

[65] OpenMP Architecture Review Board, "OpenMP application program interface version 3.0," May 2008.

[66] "Standard C++ – isocpp.org." https://isocpp.org/. [Accessed 18-01-2024].

[67] Rayon-rs, "GitHub – rayon-rs/rayon: Rayon: A data parallelism library for Rust – github.com." https://github.com/rayon-rs/rayon. [Accessed 18-01-2024].

[68] Rust, "Rust Programming Language – rust-lang.org." https://www.rust-lang.org/. [Accessed 18-01-2024].

[69] PCISIG, "Pci sig webpage," https://pcisig.com/. [Accessed 18-01-2024].

[70] NVIDIA, "NVIDIA Hopper Architecture In-Depth – NVIDIA Technical Blog – developer.nvidia.com." https://developer.nvidia.com/blog/nvidia-hopper-architecture-in-depth/. [Accessed 11-12-2023].

[71] AMD, "GitHub – ROCm/ROCm: AMD ROCm™ Software – GitHub Home – github.com." https://github.com/ROCm/ROCm. [Accessed 22-01-2024].

[72] K. Group, "OpenCL – The Open Standard for Parallel Programming of Heterogeneous Systems – khronos.org." https://www.khronos.org/opencl/. [Accessed 22-01-2024].

[73] AMD, "MI300 Series," https://www.amd.com/en/newsroom/press-releases/2023-12-6-amd-delivers-leadership-portfolio-of-data-center-a.html. [Accessed 10-12-2023].

[74] AMD, "AMD CDNA3 Architecture," https://www.amd.com/content/dam/amd/en/documents/instinct-tech-docs/white-papers/amd-cdna-3-white-paper.pdf. [Accessed 10-12-2023].

[75] N. P. Jouppi, C. Young, N. Patil, and D. Patterson, "A domain-specific architecture for deep neural networks," *Commun. ACM*, vol. 61, p. 50–59, aug 2018.

[76] R. Karanjai, S. Shin, X. Fan, L. Chen, T. Zhang, T. Suh, W. Shi, and L. Xu, "Tpu as cryptographic accelerator," 2023.

[77] "Tpu architecture," https://cloud.google.com/tpu/docs/system-architecture-tpu-vm. [Accessed 15-12-2023].

[78] A. Putnam, A. M. Caulfield, E. S. Chung, D. Chiou, K. Constantinides, J. Demme, H. Esmaeilzadeh, J. Fowers, G. P. Gopal, J. Gray, M. Haselman, S. Hauck, S. Heil, A. Hormati, J.-Y. Kim, S. Lanka, J. Larus, E. Peterson, S. Pope, A. Smith, J. Thong, P. Y. Xiao, and D. Burger, "A reconfigurable fabric for accelerating large-scale datacenter services," *IEEE Micro*, vol. 35, no. 3, pp. 10–22, 2015.

[79] NVIDIA, "NVIDIA H100 Tensor Core GPU – nvidia.com." https://www.nvidia.com/en-us/data-center/h100/. [Accessed 21-01-2024].

[80] R. T. Moenck, "Practical fast polynomial multiplication," in *Symposium on Symbolic and Algebraic Manipulation*, 1976.

[81] L. de Castro, R. Agrawal, R. Yazicigil, A. Chandrakasan, V. Vaikuntanathan, C. Juvekar, and A. Joshi, "Does fully homomorphic encryption need compute acceleration?," Cryptology ePrint Archive, Paper 2021/1636, 2021. https://eprint.iacr.org/2021/1636.

[82] N. Samardzic, A. Feldmann, A. Krastev, S. Devadas, R. Dreslinski, C. Peikert, and D. Sanchez, "F1: A fast and programmable accelerator for fully homomorphic encryption," in *MICRO-54: 54th Annual IEEE/ACM International Symposium on Microarchitecture*, MICRO '21, (New York, NY, USA), p. 238–252, Association for Computing Machinery, 2021.

[83] R. Agrawal, L. de Castro, G. Yang, C. Juvekar, R. Yazicigil, A. Chandrakasan, V. Vaikuntanathan, and A. Joshi, "Fab: An fpga-based accelerator for bootstrappable fully homomorphic encryption," in *2023 IEEE International Symposium on High-Performance Computer Architecture (HPCA)*, pp. 882–895, 2023.

[84] J. Kim, G. Lee, S. Kim, G. Sohn, M. Rhu, J. Kim, and J. H. Ahn, "Ark: Fully homomorphic encryption accelerator with runtime data generation and inter-operation key reuse," in *2022 55th IEEE/ACM International Symposium on Microarchitecture (MICRO)*, pp. 1237–1254, IEEE, 2022.

[85] A. Aikata, A. C. Mert, S. Kwon, M. Deryabin, and S. S. Roy, "Reed: Chiplet-based scalable hardware accelerator for fully homomorphic encryption," Cryptology ePrint Archive, Paper 2023/1190, 2023. https://eprint.iacr.org/2023/1190.

[86] A. Al Badawi, J. Bates, F. Bergamaschi, D. B. Cousins, S. Erabelli, N. Genise, S. Halevi, H. Hunt, A. Kim, Y. Lee, Z. Liu, D. Micciancio, I. Quah, Y. Polyakov, S. R.V., K. Rohloff, J. Saylor, D. Suponitsky, M. Triplett, V. Vaikuntanathan, and V. Zucca, "Openfhe: Open-source fully homomorphic encryption library," in *Proceedings of the 10th Workshop on Encrypted Computing & Applied Homomorphic Cryptography*, WAHC'22, (New York, NY, USA), pp. 53–63, Association for Computing Machinery, 2022.

[87] W. Jung, S. Kim, J. H. Ahn, J. H. Cheon, and Y. Lee, "Over 100x faster bootstrapping in fully homomorphic encryption through memory-centric optimization with GPUs," *IACR Transactions on Cryptographic Hardware and Embedded Systems*, pp. 114–148, Aug. 2021.

[88] S. Fan, Z. Wang, W. Xu, R. Hou, D. Meng, and M. Zhang, "Tensorfhe: Achieving practical computation on encrypted data using gpgpu," in *2023 IEEE International Symposium on High-Performance Computer Architecture (HPCA)*, (Los Alamitos, CA, USA), pp. 922–934, IEEE Computer Society, mar 2023.

[89] K. Shivdikar, Y. Bao, R. Agrawal, M. Shen, G. Jonatan, E. Mora, A. Ingare, N. Livesay, J. L. AbellÁN, J. Kim, A. Joshi, and D. Kaeli, "Gme: Gpu-based microarchitectural extensions to accelerate homomorphic encryption," in *Proceedings of the 56th Annual IEEE/ACM International Symposium on Microarchitecture*, MICRO '23, (New York, NY, USA), p. 670–684, Association for Computing Machinery, 2023.

[90] Y. Bao, Y. Sun, Z. Feric, M. T. Shen, M. Weston, J. L. Abellán, T. Baruah, J. Kim, A. Joshi, and D. Kaeli, "Navisim: A highly accurate gpu simulator for amd rdna gpus," in *Proceedings of the International Conference on Parallel Architectures and Compilation Techniques*, PACT '22, (New York, NY, USA), p. 333–345, Association for Computing Machinery, 2023.

[91] G. Lee, M. Kim, J. H. Park, S.-w. Hwang, and J. H. Cheon, "Privacy-preserving text classification on BERT embeddings with homomorphic encryption," in *Proceedings of the 2022 Conference of the North American Chapter of the Association for Computational Linguistics: Human Language Technologies* (M. Carpuat, M.-C. de Marneffe, and I. V. Meza Ruiz, eds.), (Seattle, United States), pp. 3169–3175, Association for Computational Linguistics, July 2022.

[92] I. Chillotti, M. Joye, and P. Paillier, "Programmable bootstrapping enables efficient homomorphic inference of deep neural networks," in *Cyber Security Cryptography and Machine Learning* (S. Dolev, O. Margalit, B. Pinkas, and A. Schwarzmann, eds.), (Cham), pp. 1–19, Springer International Publishing, 2021.

[93] Zama, "Concrete: TFHE Compiler that converts python programs into FHE equivalent," 2022. https://github.com/zama-ai/concrete.

[94] T. K. Ho, "Random decision forests," in *Proceedings of 3rd International Conference on Document Analysis and Recognition*, vol. 1, pp. 278–282, 1995.

[95] dmlc, "GitHub – dmlc/xgboost: Scalable, Portable and Distributed Gradient Boosting (GBDT, GBRT or GBM) Library, for Python, R, Java, Scala, C++ and more. Runs on single machine, Hadoop, Spark, Dask, Flink and DataFlow – github.com." https://github.com/dmlc/xgboost. [Accessed 22-01-2024].

[96] S. Russell and P. Norvig, *Artificial Intelligence: A Modern Approach*. Pearson, 4th ed., 2020.

[97] A. Radford, J. Wu, R. Child, D. Luan, D. Amodei, and I. Sutskever, "Language models are unsupervised multitask learners," 2019.

[98] T. B. Brown, B. Mann, N. Ryder, M. Subbiah, J. Kaplan, P. Dhariwal, A. Neelakantan, P. Shyam, G. Sastry, A. Askell, S. Agarwal, A. Herbert-Voss, G. Krueger, T. Henighan, R. Child, A. Ramesh, D. M. Ziegler, J. Wu,

C. Winter, C. Hesse, M. Chen, E. Sigler, M. Litwin, S. Gray, B. Chess, J. Clark, C. Berner, S. McCandlish, A. Radford, I. Sutskever, and D. Amodei, "Language models are few-shot learners," 2020.

[99] A. Putra, Prasetiyo, Y. Chen, J. Kim, and J.-Y. Kim, "Strix: An end-to-end streaming architecture with two-level ciphertext batching for fully homomorphic encryption with programmable bootstrapping," in *Proceedings of the 56th Annual IEEE/ACM International Symposium on Microarchitecture*, MICRO '23, (New York, NY, USA), p. 1319–1331, Association for Computing Machinery, 2023.

[100] Nucypher, "Nucypher/nufhe: Nucypher fully homomorphic encryption (nufhe) library implemented in python."

[101] L. Jiang, Q. Lou, and N. Joshi, "MATCHA: a fast and energy-efficient accelerator for fully homomorphic encryption over the torus," in *DAC '22: 59th ACM/IEEE Design Automation Conference, San Francisco, California, USA, July 10–14, 2022* (R. Oshana, ed.), pp. 235–240, ACM, 2022.

[102] I. Chillotti, M. Joye, and P. Paillier, "Programmable bootstrapping enables efficient homomorphic inference of deep neural networks," in *Cyber Security Cryptography and Machine Learning* (S. Dolev, O. Margalit, B. Pinkas, and A. Schwarzmann, eds.), (Cham), pp. 1–19, Springer International Publishing, 2021.

[103] vernamlab, "GitHub – vernamlab/cuFHE: CUDA-accelerated Fully Homomorphic Encryption Library – github.com." https://github.com/vernamlab /cuFHE. [Accessed 22-01-2024].

[104] Z. AI, "Announcing concrete-core v1.0.0-gamma with gpu acceleration."

[105] A. Kolesnikov, A. Dosovitskiy, D. Weissenborn, G. Heigold, J. Uszkoreit, L. Beyer, M. Minderer, M. Dehghani, N. Houlsby, S. Gelly, T. Unterthiner, and X. Zhai, "An image is worth 16x16 words: Transformers for image recognition at scale," 2021.

[106] A. Vaswani, N. M. Shazeer, N. Parmar, J. Uszkoreit, L. Jones, A. N. Gomez, L. Kaiser, and I. Polosukhin, "Attention is all you need," in *Neural Information Processing Systems*, 2017.

[107] X. Zhou, Z. Xu, C. Wang, and M. X. Gao, "Ppmlac: high performance chipset architecture for secure multi-party computation," *Proceedings of the 49th Annual International Symposium on Computer Architecture*, 2022.

[108] A. Waterman, Y. Lee, D. A. Patterson, and K. Asanović, "The risc-v instruction set manual, volume i: User-level isa, version 2.0," Tech. Rep. UCB/EECS-2014-54, EECS Department, University of California, Berkeley, May 2014.

[109] R. Patel, P. Haghi, S. Jain, A. Kot, V. Krishnan, M. Varia, and M. Herbord, "Distributed hardware accelerated secure joint computation on the copa framework," in *2022 IEEE High Performance Extreme Computing Conference (HPEC)*, pp. 1–7, 2022.

[110] V. Krishnan, O. Serres, and M. Blocksome, "Configurable network protocol accelerator (copa): An integrated networking/accelerator hardware/software framework," in *2020 IEEE Symposium on High-Performance Interconnects (HOTI)*, pp. 17–24, 2020.

[111] A. Dalskov, D. E. Escudero, and M. Keller, "Fantastic four: Honest-majority four-party secure computation with malicious security," *IACR Cryptol. ePrint Arch.*, vol. 2020, p. 1330, 2020.

[112] "Q3 2023 Data Breach Report." https://www.idtheftcenter.org/post/q3-20 23-data-breach-report-itrc-reports-data-compromise-record-with-three-m onths-left-in-year/. [Accessed 07-01-2024].

[113] "Cost of a data breach 2023 – IBM – ibm.com." https://www.ibm.com/re ports/data-breach. [Accessed 07-01-2024].

[114] Onai, "Award #2028008 – sbir phase i: Accelerating understanding of covid-19 biology and treatment via scaled medical record and biosimulation analytics," https://www.nsf.gov/awardsearch/showAward?AWD_ID=2028008, 2020.

[115] A. Khedr and G. Gulak, "Securemed: Secure medical computation using gpu-accelerated homomorphic encryption scheme," *IEEE Journal of Biomedical and Health Informatics*, vol. 22, no. 2, pp. 597–606, 2018.

[116] J. Hoffstein, J. Pipher, and J. H. Silverman, "Ntru: A ring-based public key cryptosystem," in *Algorithmic Number Theory* (J. P. Buhler, ed.), (Berlin, Heidelberg), pp. 267–288, Springer Berlin Heidelberg, 1998.

[117] P. W. Wilson, R. B. D'Agostino, D. Levy, A. M. Belanger, H. Silbershatz, and W. B. Kannel, "Prediction of coronary heart disease using risk factor categories," *Circulation*, vol. 97, pp. 1837–1847, May 1998.

[118] J. Chao, A. A. Badawi, B. Unnikrishnan, J. Lin, C. F. Mun, J. M. Brown, J. P. Campbell, M. Chiang, J. Kalpathy-Cramer, V. R. Chandrasekhar, P. Krishnaswamy, and K. M. M. Aung, "Carenets: Compact and resource-efficient cnn for homomorphic inference on encrypted medical images," 2019.

[119] R. Gilad-Bachrach, N. Dowlin, K. Laine, K. Lauter, M. Naehrig, and J. Wernsing, "Cryptonets: Applying neural networks to encrypted data with high throughput and accuracy," in *Proceedings of The 33rd International Conference on Machine Learning* (M. F. Balcan and K. Q. Weinberger, eds.), vol. 48 of *Proceedings of Machine Learning Research*, (New York, New York, USA), pp. 201–210, PMLR, 20–22 Jun 2016.

[120] H. Smajlović, A. Shajii, B. Berger, H. Cho, and I. Numanagić, "Sequre: a high-performance framework for secure multiparty computation enables biomedical data sharing," *Genome Biology*, vol. 24, no. 1, p. 5, 2023.

[121] A. Ziller, A. Trask, A. Lopardo, B. Szymkow, B. Wagner, E. Bluemke, J.-M. Nounahon, J. Passerat-Palmbach, K. Prakash, N. Rose, *et al.*, "Pysyft: A library for easy federated learning," *Federated Learning Systems: Towards Next-Generation AI*, pp. 111–139, 2021.

[122] G. Spini, E. Mancini, T. Attema, M. Abspoel, J. de Gier, S. Fehr, T. Veugen, M. van Heesch, D. Worm, A. De Luca, R. Cramer, and P. M. A. Sloot, "New approach to privacy-preserving clinical decision support systems for HIV treatment," *J. Med. Syst.*, vol. 46, p. 84, Oct. 2022.

[123] B. Hie, H. Cho, and B. Berger, "Realizing private and practical pharmacological collaboration," *Science*, vol. 362, no. 6412, pp. 347–350, 2018.

[124] R. Ma, Y. Li, C. Li, F. Wan, H. Hu, W. Xu, and J. Zeng, "Secure multiparty computation for privacy-preserving drug discovery," *Bioinformatics (Oxford, England)*, vol. 36, pp. 2872–2880, May 2020.

[125] Y. Li and W. Xu, "Privpy: General and scalable privacy-preserving data mining," in *Proceedings of the 25th ACM SIGKDD International Conference on Knowledge Discovery & Data Mining*, pp. 1299–1307, 2019.

[126] C. A. Morillo, A. Banerjee, P. Perel, D. Wood, and X. Jouven, "Atrial fibrillation: the current epidemic," *J. Geriatr. Cardiol.*, vol. 14, pp. 195–203, Mar. 2017.

[127] A. Vizitiu, C.-I. Nita, R. M. Toev, T. Suditu, C. Suciu, and L. M. Itu, "Framework for privacy-preserving wearable health data analysis: Proof-of-concept study for atrial fibrillation detection," *Applied Sciences*, vol. 11, no. 19, 2021.

[128] A. L. Goldberger, L. A. N. Amaral, L. Glass, J. M. Hausdorff, P. C. Ivanov, R. G. Mark, J. E. Mietus, G. B. Moody, C.-K. Peng, and H. E. Stanley, "Physiobank, physiotoolkit, and physionet," *Circulation*, vol. 101, no. 23, pp. e215–e220, 2000.

[129] A. Kipnis and E. Hibshoosh, "Efficient methods for practical fully homomorphic symmetric-key encrypton, randomization and verification," *IACR Cryptol. ePrint Arch.*, vol. 2012, p. 637, 2012.

[130] R. Tanwar, N. Nandal, M. Zamani, and A. A. Manaf, "Pathway of trends and technologies in fall detection: A systematic review," *Healthcare (Basel)*, vol. 10, p. 172, Jan. 2022.

[131] P. Mainali and C. Shepherd, "Privacy-enhancing fall detection from remote sensor data using multi-party computation," *Proceedings of the 14th International Conference on Availability, Reliability and Security*, 2019.

[132] T. Mauldin, M. Canby, V. Metsis, A. Ngu, and C. Rivera, "SmartFall: A smartwatch-based fall detection system using deep learning," *Sensors (Basel)*, vol. 18, p. 3363, Oct. 2018.

[133] "GitHub – lschoe/mpyc: MPyC: Multiparty Computation in Python – github.com." https://github.com/lschoe/mpyc. [Accessed 08-01-2024].

[134] FTC.gov, "Ring's privacy failures led to spying and harassment through home security cameras," https://consumer.ftc.gov/consumer-alerts/202 3/05/rings-privacy-failures-led-spying-and-harassment-through-home-sec urity-cameras. [Accessed 08-01-2024].

[135] X. Jin, H. Zhang, X. Li, H. Yu, B. Liu, S. Xie, A. K. Singh, and Y. Li, "Confused-modulo-projection-based somewhat homomorphic encryption—cryptosystem, library, and applications on secure smart cities," *IEEE Internet of Things Journal*, vol. 8, pp. 6324–6336, 2020.

[136] X. Li, H. Gao, J. Zhang, S. Yang, X. Jin, and K.-K. R. Choo, "Gpu accelerated full homomorphic encryption cryptosystem, library and applications for iot systems," *IEEE Internet of Things Journal*, pp. 1–1, 2023.

[137] Z. Azad, G. Yang, R. Agrawal, D. Petrisko, M. Taylor, and A. Joshi, "Rise: Risc-v soc for en/decryption acceleration on the edge for homomorphic encryption," *IEEE Transactions on Very Large Scale Integration (VLSI) Systems*, vol. PP, pp. 1–14, 10 2023.

[138] F. Krieger, F. Hirner, A. C. Mert, and S. S. Roy, "Aloha-he: A low-area hardware accelerator for client-side operations in homomorphic encryption," Cryptology ePrint Archive, Paper 2023/1736, 2023. https://eprint.iacr. org/2023/1736.

[139] D. Chaum, *Computer Systems Established, Maintained and Trusted by Mutually Suspicious Groups*. University of California, Berkeley, 1982.

[140] S. Nakamoto, "Bitcoin: A peer-to-peer electronic cash system," Dec 2008.

[141] S. Goldwasser, S. Micali, and C. Rackoff, "The knowledge complexity of interactive proof-systems," in *Proceedings of the Seventeenth Annual ACM Symposium on Theory of Computing*, STOC '85, (New York, NY, USA), p. 291–304, Association for Computing Machinery, 1985.

[142] E. Ben-Sasson, A. Chiesa, M. Riabzev, N. Spooner, M. Virza, and N. P. Ward, "Aurora: Transparent succinct arguments for r1cs," in *Advances in Cryptology – EUROCRYPT 2019* (Y. Ishai and V. Rijmen, eds.), (Cham), pp. 103–128, Springer International Publishing, 2019.

[143] "Zcash: Privacy-protecting digital currency – z.cash," https://z.cash/. [Accessed 14-01-2024].

[144] N. Szabo, "Formalizing and securing relationships on public networks," *First Monday*, vol. 2, Sep. 1997.

[145] A. J. Menezes, S. A. Vanstone, and P. C. V. Oorschot, *Handbook of Applied Cryptography*. USA: CRC Press, Inc., 1st ed., 1996.

[146] P. Rogaway and T. Shrimpton, "Cryptographic hash-function basics: Definitions, implications, and separations for preimage resistance, second-preimage resistance, and collision resistance," in *Fast Software Encryption* (B. Roy and W. Meier, eds.), (Berlin, Heidelberg), pp. 371–388, Springer Berlin Heidelberg, 2004.

[147] E. Ben-Sasson, L. Goldberg, and D. Levit, "Stark friendly hash – survey and recommendation," Cryptology ePrint Archive, Paper 2020/948, 2020. https://eprint.iacr.org/2020/948.

[148] J. Thaler *et al.*, "Proofs, arguments, and zero-knowledge," *Foundations and Trends® in Privacy and Security*, vol. 4, no. 2–4, pp. 117–660, 2022.

[149] J. Groth, "On the size of pairing-based non-interactive arguments," in *Advances in Cryptology – EUROCRYPT 2016* (M. Fischlin and J.-S. Coron, eds.), (Berlin, Heidelberg), pp. 305–326, Springer Berlin Heidelberg, 2016.

[150] E. Ben-Sasson, I. Bentov, Y. Horesh, and M. Riabzev, "Scalable, transparent, and post-quantum secure computational integrity," *IACR Cryptol. ePrint Arch.*, p. 46, 2018.

[151] A. Kothapalli, S. Setty, and I. Tzialla, "Nova: Recursive zero-knowledge arguments from folding schemes," in *Advances in Cryptology – CRYPTO 2022* (Y. Dodis and T. Shrimpton, eds.), (Cham), pp. 359–388, Springer Nature Switzerland, 2022.

[152] "Ethereum Whitepaper – ethereum.org – ethereum.org." https://ethereum.org/en/whitepaper. [Accessed 14-01-2024].

[153] "Loopring – zkRollup Layer 2 for Trading and Payment – loopring.org." https://loopring.org/#/. [Accessed 14-01-2024].

[154] Noir, "GitHub – noir-lang/noir: Noir is a domain specific language for zero knowledge proofs – github.com." https://github.com/noir-lang/noir, 2021.

[155] Zokrates, "GitHub – Zokrates/ZoKrates: A toolbox for zkSNARKs on Ethereum – github.com." https://github.com/Zokrates/ZoKrates, 2019.

[156] iden3, "GitHub – iden3/circom: zkSnark circuit compiler – github.com." https://github.com/iden3/circom, 2022.

[157] "Cairo – cairo-lang.org." https://www.cairo-lang.org/. [Accessed 15-01-2024].

[158] "RISC Zero : General-Purpose Verifiable Computing – risczero.com." https://www.risczero.com/. [Accessed 15-01-2024].

[159] facebook, "GitHub – facebook/winterfell: A STARK prover and verifier for arbitrary computations – github.com." https://github.com/facebook/winterfell. [Accessed 15-01-2024].

[160] ingonyama zk, "GitHub – ingonyama-zk/icicle: a GPU Library for Zero-Knowledge Acceleration – github.com." https://github.com/ingonyama-zk/icicle. [Accessed 15-01-2024].

[161] filecoin project, "GitHub – filecoin-project/bellperson: zk-SNARK library – github.com." https://github.com/filecoin-project/bellperson. [Accessed 15-01-2024].

[162] zkcrypto, "GitHub – zkcrypto/bellman: zk-SNARK library. – github.com." https://github.com/zkcrypto/bellman. [Accessed 15-01-2024].

[163] zkonduit, "GitHub – zkonduit/ezkl: ezkl is an engine for doing inference for deep learning models and other computational graphs in a zk-snark (ZKML). Use it from Python, Javascript, or the command line. – github.com." https://github.com/zkonduit/ezkl. [Accessed 15-01-2024].

[164] Ingonyama, "ZPU: The Zero-Knowledge Processing Unit – ingonyama." https://medium.com/@ingonyama/zpu-the-zero-knowledge-processing-unit-f886a48e00e0. [Accessed 15-01-2024].

[165] Y. Zhang, S. Wang, X. Zhang, J. Dong, X. Mao, F. Long, C. Wang, D. Zhou, M. Gao, and G. Sun, "Pipezk: Accelerating zero-knowledge proof with a pipelined architecture," in *2021 ACM/IEEE 48th Annual International Symposium on Computer Architecture (ISCA)*, pp. 416–428, 2021.

[166] A. Ali, B. A. S. Al-rimy, F. S. Alsubaei, A. A. Almazroi, and A. A. Almazroi, "Healthlock: Blockchain-based privacy preservation using homomorphic encryption in internet of things healthcare applications," *Sensors*, vol. 23, no. 15, 2023.

[167] R. A. Fisher, "Iris." UCI Machine Learning Repository, 1988. DOI: https://doi.org/10.24432/C56C76.

[168] B. Zhang, G. Lu, P. Qiu, X. Gui, and Y. Shi, "Advancing federated learning through verifiable computations and homomorphic encryption," *Entropy*, vol. 25, no. 11, 2023.

Index

About the Authors

The authors contribute at Onai Inc. to the advancement of accelerated privacy-preserving artificial intelligence.

Jayavanth Shenoy develops and integrates sophisticated software solutions for highly advanced, performant, distributed network systems, focusing on acceleration of cryptographic and artificial intelligence applications. He is an expert in privacy-preserving AI and also has extensive experience in high performance computing.

Patrick Grinaway earned his doctorate in the Chodera Lab of the Weill Cornell Medical College of Cornell University. He conducted work on advanced statistical sampling methods for biomedical computation and on distributed computing. He has expertise in artificial intelligence, cryptography, and drug discovery.

Shriphani Palakodety holds expertise in machine learning methods, notably for sensitive or difficult-to-access data, and blockchain systems. He has published at top venues in artificial intelligence and natural language processing, including AAAI, EMNLP, and IJCAI. He co-authored the book Low Resource Social Media Text Mining.

Milton Keynes UK
Ingram Content Group UK Ltd.
UKHW052201160424
441169UK00002B/5

9 781638 283447